S0-AFO-101

DUNNINGER'S BOOK OF MAGIC

by Joseph Dunninger

Bonanza Books • New York

Thanks is herewith extended to Gernsback Publications for permission to include the material in this volume which originally appeared under the author's byline in "Science and Invention" and "Everyday Science and Mechanics."

This book was originally included in *Dunninger's Monument to Magic.*

This edition is published by Bonanza Books,
a division of Crown Publishers, Inc.,
by arrangement with Lyle Stuart, Inc.
a b c d e f g h
BONANZA 1979 EDITION
Manufactured in the United States of America

Library of Congress Cataloging in Publication Data
Dunninger, Joseph, 1896-1975
Dunninger's book of magic.
"Originally included in Dunninger's monument to magic."
1. Conjuring. 2. Tricks. 3. Dunninger, Joseph, 1896- 4. Magicians—United States—Biography. I. Title. II. Title: Book of magic.
GV1547.D748 1979 '793.8 79-14851
ISBN 0-517-29306-4

CONTENTS

A Dunninger Scrapbook

INTRODUCTION

Among the "Greats" of modern magic, the name of Dunninger stands above all. I say this with authority, because it has been my good fortune and great privilege to be associated both as a confidant and writer with all the great magicians of America since the first decade of this century. To be more precise, the year 1910, and if it seems odd to specify it that exactly, I have a good reason for doing so. It was then that I witnessed a performance of Dunninger at the famous Eden Musee in New York City. He was the first great stage magician I had ever seen.

I have followed his career ever since, watching his inimitable performances over a span of sixty years; and by a strange coincidence – or perhaps by a quirk of fate! – he is the last of all those great magicians whose work I have watched. Even today he is always ready to present some of the unfathomable marvels or near-miracles that made him famous.

In those early days, he was known as "The Mysterious Dunninger." Today he is billed as "The Amazing Dunninger." In all the decades between, he has never termed himself "The World's Greatest Magician," though he would have more right to that title than many who have claimed it. Yet he has never criticized others for using it, for he has always felt that it is an honor that should be shared. Some of these magicians have presented their own full evening shows; others have appeared in vaudeville; still more have worked in night clubs. There have been Handcuff Kings, Card Kings, Coin Kings, and Silk Kings, as well as masters of close-up wizardry. All deserve their respective niches in Magic's Hall of Fame.

The factor that places Dunninger high on the list, and at the same time renders him unique, is his fantastic versatility. When handcuff acts were still in vogue, Dunninger was recognized as one of the country's leading escape artists. As a sleight-of-hand performer, he rapidly rose to the top rank and has maintained that status ever since. He became a pioneer in the field of hypnotism as the first performer to hypnotize a person over radio. He toured America from coast to coast with his own company in a full-evening magic show, appearing in leading theaters in the largest cities at a time when big shows were in their heyday. As a vaudeville headliner, he shattered house records both as an illusionist and a master mentalist.

When fraudulent spirit mediums were gulling the American public, Dunninger vied with Houdini in exposing their pretended miracles. After Houdini's untimely death, Dunninger carried on this work alone, under such notable auspices as the Scientific American and the Universal Council for Psychical Research.

Still greater was Dunninger's fame in the field of mentalism, where he introduced his one man mind-reading act, unaided by assistants. He offered a standing award to anyone who could prove that he used paid confederates. His appearances in society circles brought him the highest fees ever paid a mystifier for an individual performance. When his act was adapted to radio, over a national network in the presence of regular studio audiences, it became the sensation of the airwaves. With the advent of television, Dunninger was one of the few great radio stars who became an even greater sensation in this new phase of broadcasting, for the simple reason that his masterful demonstrations could now be seen as well as heard. It brought viewers throughout the nation the opportunity of observing Dunninger's inimitable marvels at the closest possible range.

All this stands as tribute to Dunninger's versatility, which in turn bears out the fact that he has one of the most inventive minds in magic, having created and improved literally thousands of magical effects throughout his long and arduous lifetime. Where other "Greats" have been content to stay with their set routines or more famous illusions, Dunninger has constantly been adding to his repertoire.

His versatility has an important bearing on this book, for Dunninger, due to the productivity of his ingenious mind, has always been willing, in fact eager, to share his secrets of magic with newcomers in the craft. The logic behind this is sound indeed. With the rapid advance of modern scientific knowledge, many traditional feats of magic have truly become "old hat" where sophisticated audiences are concerned. Hence the only way to keep the art alive is to supplant timeworn methods with new and more baffling devices. Dunninger has done this not only on the stage and over the air, but in the literary field as well.

Years ago, Dunninger compiled three volumes of "Popular Magic" which for variety, comprehensive coverage, and illustrative effect have remained unequalled. Sought by magical collectors everywhere, they became such rarities that they were combined and published by Lyle Stuart as *Dunninger's Complete Encyclopedia of Magic,* which has continued to top the best-seller list in its field. During the same years when "Popular Magic" appeared, Dunninger also supplied monthly articles on magic to such magazines as *Science and Invention* and *Everyday Science and Mechanics.*

This newer material, which never appeared in book form, was still more difficult to acquire. So now, it has been combined with other of Dunninger's magical writings to form the present volume. Magic is fortunate indeed to have Dunninger as one of its Greats.

1974 *Walter B. Gibson*

Walter B. Gibson, creator of Lamont Cranston, the Shadow

Dunninger Biography

Joseph Dunninger, the Master Mind whose mental wizardry has baffled scientists and psychologists throughout the world, was a native New Yorker. He made his home in Cliffside Park, New Jersey, across the Hudson River, not far from the district in which he spent his boyhood days and near the home of many of his old friends, who are still his most esteemed critics.

Apparently Dunninger's mysterious "master mind" was not a case of heredity. His father was a successful Bavarian textile manufacturer, and his mother performed the duties of a housewife in a purely mundane manner. Nor did his brothers have any link with the world of magic; one became a concert violinist and the other a painter and designer.

But in Joseph there was awakened a yearning toward magic feats even at the age of five, when he showed a marked ability at sleight-of-hand. His parents encouraged this novelty; much amused they were at his dexterity in simple palming tricks. Self-taught, Dunninger soon had a remarkable repertoire of necromancy. His childhood pastime earned him an invitation to appear before a Masonic Club at the age of seven, where he was billed as "Master Joseph Dunninger, Child Magician."

It was at this time that he caused some wonderment among his school teachers. Master Joseph did not seem to be an extra brilliant pupil, but he invariably got all his arithmetic problems correct. Could it be that he copied the answers from bright children seated near him? His seating place in the classroom was frequently changed, but still Joseph's papers were marked 100 percent.

Dunninger explained it: "You see, I just couldn't get the wrong answer; I didn't have to work the problems out. The bright children in the classroom just sent me thought waves, and consequently I got everything right."

By the time that Dunninger was sixteen, he was an adult magician with an enviable reputation, and appeared for a year at the famous Eden Musee in 23rd Street. The Boy Dunninger outmastered many of the most prominent prestidigitators of the day, and this launched him on a vaudeville tour. It was during this tour that he developed the astounding stunt of reading the minds of members of his audiences. For many years actors had presented such an illusion through the means of code messages between an assistant in the audience and the "thought reader" on the stage. Dunninger used no assistants and never found it necessary to do so. In fact, he had a standing offer of $10,000 to anyone who could prove that he used confederates or "stooges." Dunninger said he could raise that offer to $100,000. No one ever collected it because he did not need assistance.

Dunninger headlined throughout the Keith-Orpheum Circuit and was much in demand for private entertainment. At the age of seventeen he was invited to perform at the home of Theodore Roosevelt in Oyster Bay and at the home of the inventor Thomas A. Edison, both of whom were avid admirers of his mysticism. It was during this association that Dunninger developed some of the remarkable experiments that he used in his performance.

His ability to read thoughts amazed the great Harry Houdini, and Howard Thurston went to great length in his search for the secret of Dunninger's mental wizardry. It was in this association that Dunninger took up his campaign of "illusion busting" waged against fraudulent mediums who had grown rich by falsification of seances that were designed to make people believe that word can come back from the spirit world. Through the Scientific American Magazine and the University Council for Psychic Research, Dunninger offered $10,000 to any medium who could produce by psychic or supernatural means any physical phenomenon that he could not reproduce by natural means or explain in convincing materialistic terms.

He offered that amount of money to anyone who, with astral aid, could disclose the translation of secret code messages entrusted to him by the late Harry Houdini and Thomas A. Edison, both of whom wanted to investigate the possibilities of communication with spirits. Dunninger also offered $10,000 to anyone who could introduce to him a real house-haunting ghost.

Most the big-time vaudeville houses in the country boasted of having Dunninger on their stages in those days. Before long his "single" became a troupe of fifty with "Dunninger, the Master Mind of Mental Mystery," presenting a full evening's entertainment, which included all manner of amazing illusions. Many of the acts he created have never been accomplished by another, and he was also responsible for the presence of many startling features in the repertoire of magicians now appearing before the public today. It is said that Dunninger created more illusions than any other inventor of this type of entertainment.

He toured the world East and West, reading the thoughts of princes and Pope Pius XII and had been invited to the White House six times for presidential parties at which times he read the minds of the presidents.

When commercial radio started, Dunninger made his air debut in a demonstration of hypnosis by radio. He was next heard in the role of psychic detective. But neither of these features caught on. It was Daniel S. Tuthill who successfully evolved the Dunninger radio-formula—thought reading. The idea quickly caught the favor of Phillips Carlin, at that time Vice President of the American Broadcasting Company, and on September 12, 1943, Dunninger's first broadcast as "Dunninger, the Master Mind" was produced.

The studio audience went wild with excitement; letters poured in from listeners all over the country and radio editors pounded away at their typewriters. Awards and citations publicized the program. Celebrities in all fields of endeavor offered their time and brains to serve as guest judges. The show was sustaining for only a few months before Sherwin Williams Paint Company stepped in as sponsor for 52 weeks. When Dunninger went on a coast-to-coast tour, the broadcasts emanated from cities en route. Twenty-six national magazines published feature stories on Dunninger's remarkable talent. Dunninger wrote the book *What's on Your Mind?* and 100,000 copies were sold in approximately six months.

Since then Dunninger completed two more radio series, both for Lever Brothers, over the facilities of the National Broadcasting Company network. In June 1946 he made another debut—his first nightly engagement in a hotel. For eight weeks he appeared at the stroke of midnight in the Cascades Room of the Hotel Biltmore in New York City and read the thoughts of the guests. During his stay at the Biltmore, he broke all attendance records at the Cascades Room for thirty-one years!

He invaded television in 1948 under the sponsorship of Bigelow-Sanford carpets and for two years was one of the most popular artists on television. For seven years the great Dunninger appeared on a television series for Hazel Bishop and for Pall Mall Division of the American Tobacco Company.

Dunninger and F.D. Roosevelt

Joseph Dunninger, generally regarded as the world's premiere mentalist and mindreader was born in New York City on April 18, 1892. At the time of Dunninger's birth Houdini was 18 years old. However, in later years the younger Dunninger and Houdini were to become very close associates.

In addition to his success as a mental wizard Dunninger also developed a considerable reputation as the inventor and designer of many spectacular illusions and sensations which were performed by the great magicians of his day, including Houdini.

In 1926 Dunninger acquired many of the effects seen in the Museum from the Houdini estate. To a large extent the equipment was relegated to a warehouse in New York where it remained for almost a half century, at which time it became available to the Houdini Museum.

Dunninger's fame as a mentalist gained him an audience with royalty, and several of the U.S. Presidents. Perhaps one of Dunninger's most sensational encounters took place with F. D. Roosevelt prior to his election as President of the United States. The amazing Dunninger asked the President-to-be to write any question to which he wished an answer on a piece of paper. Without seeing the question Dunninger recorded the reply on his slate. One can imagine Roosevelt's startled reaction when Dunninger showed him in the written answer, "You will be President" as his reply to Roosevelt's question, "Who will be the next President?"

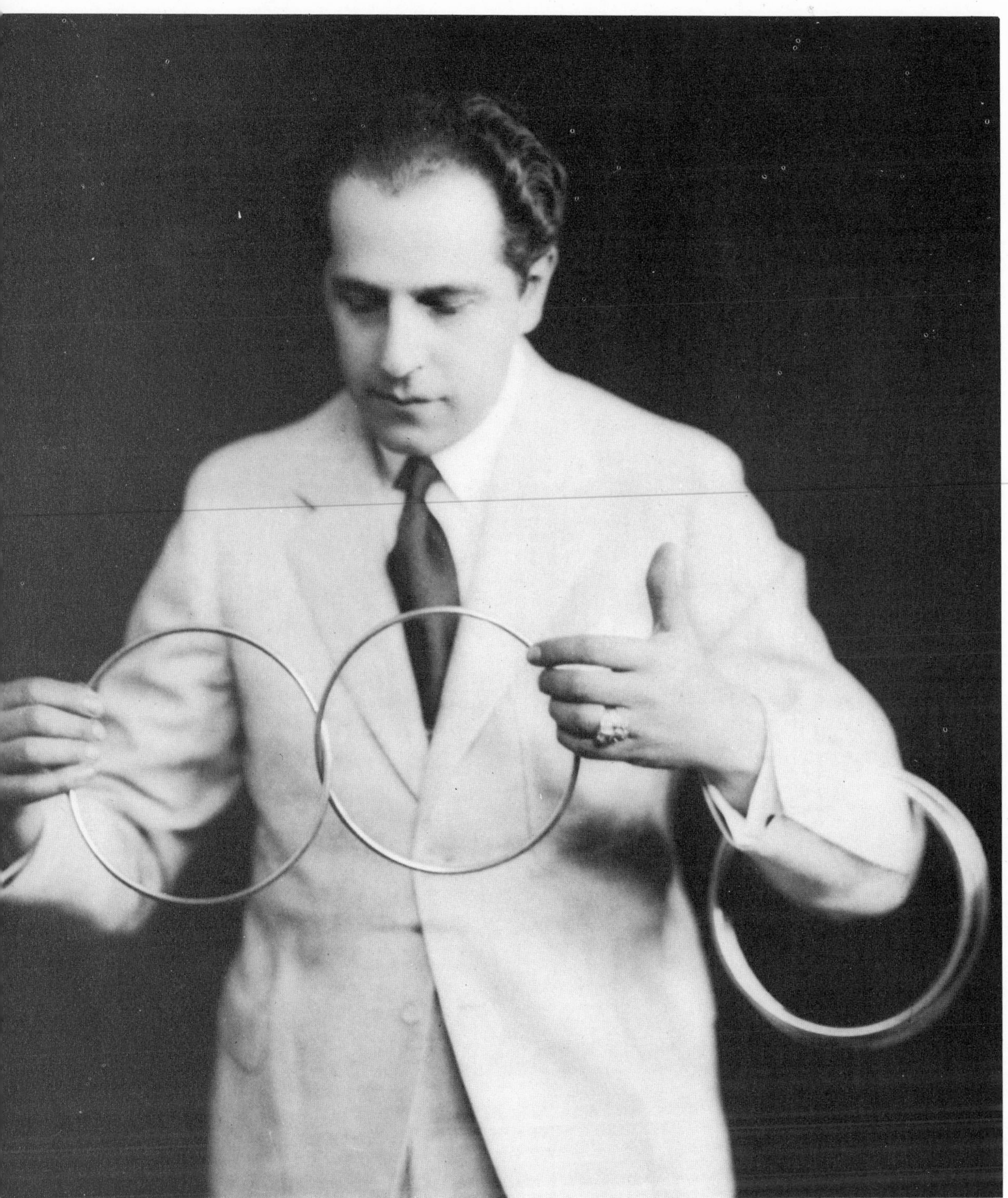

An early photo of Dunninger

Dunninger demonstrating a card trick for Tony Curtis, Janet Leigh and Jerry Lewis

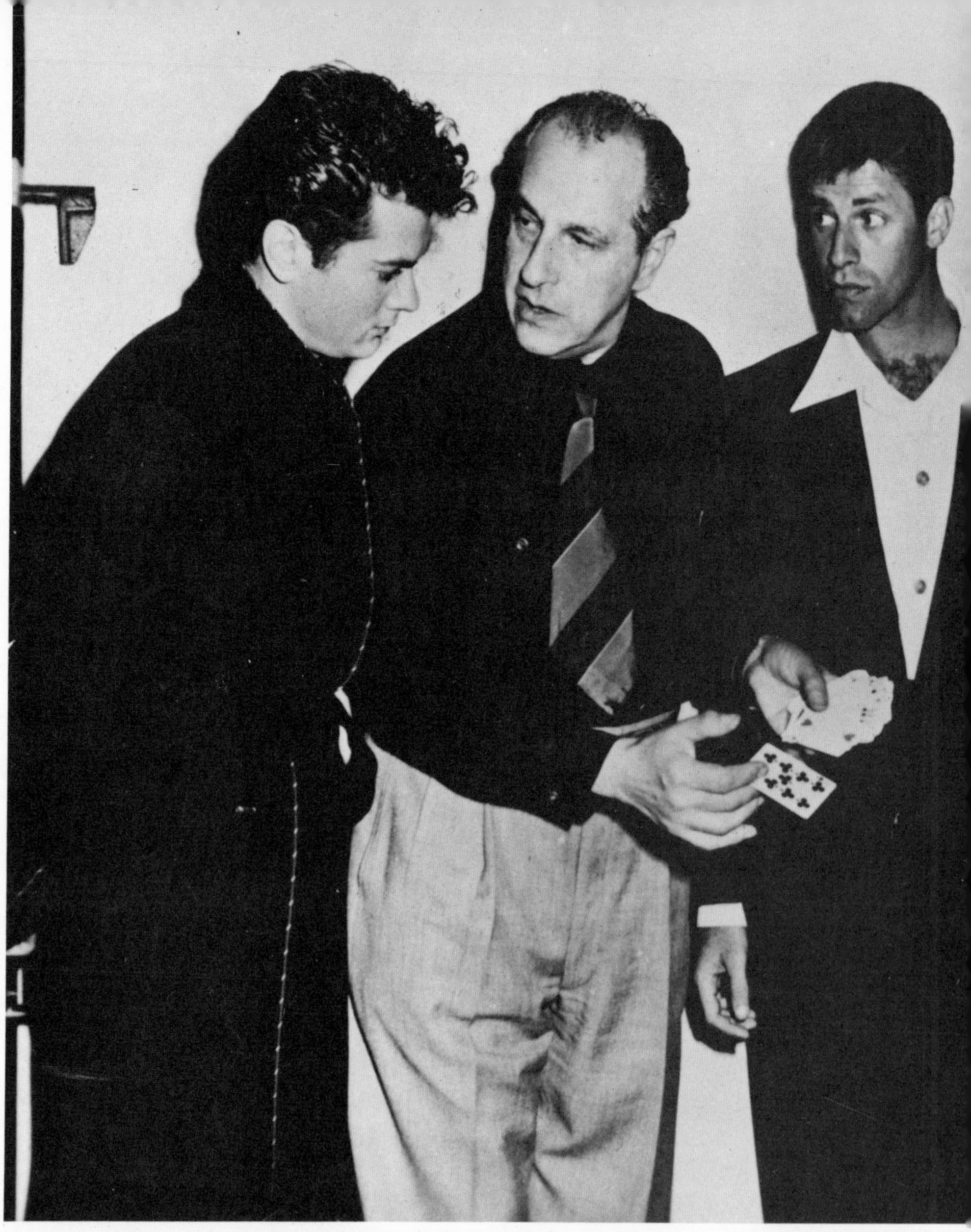

With Bob Hope

A note from movie stars Tony Curtis and Janet Leigh to Dunninger, who was technical advisor to the Paramount Pictures's film *Houdini*.

Janet and Tony

Dear Joe!

I would need a Volume of Blank Paper to Express our Deep appreciation for your +.

ind help
d assistance to
ry to make me look
like an accomplished
magician. For Everything
you've done Dear Joe
God Bless You and
Keep You for your
truly the Great
Dunninger

Love Janet and Tony

Dunninger demonstrates hypnotism before a group of more than five hundred eminent physicians and surgeons. The subject, suspended over the backs of two chairs, is in a cataleptic state. Dunninger is credited with many phenomenal hypnotic cures, which have been acknowledged by doctors throughout the country.

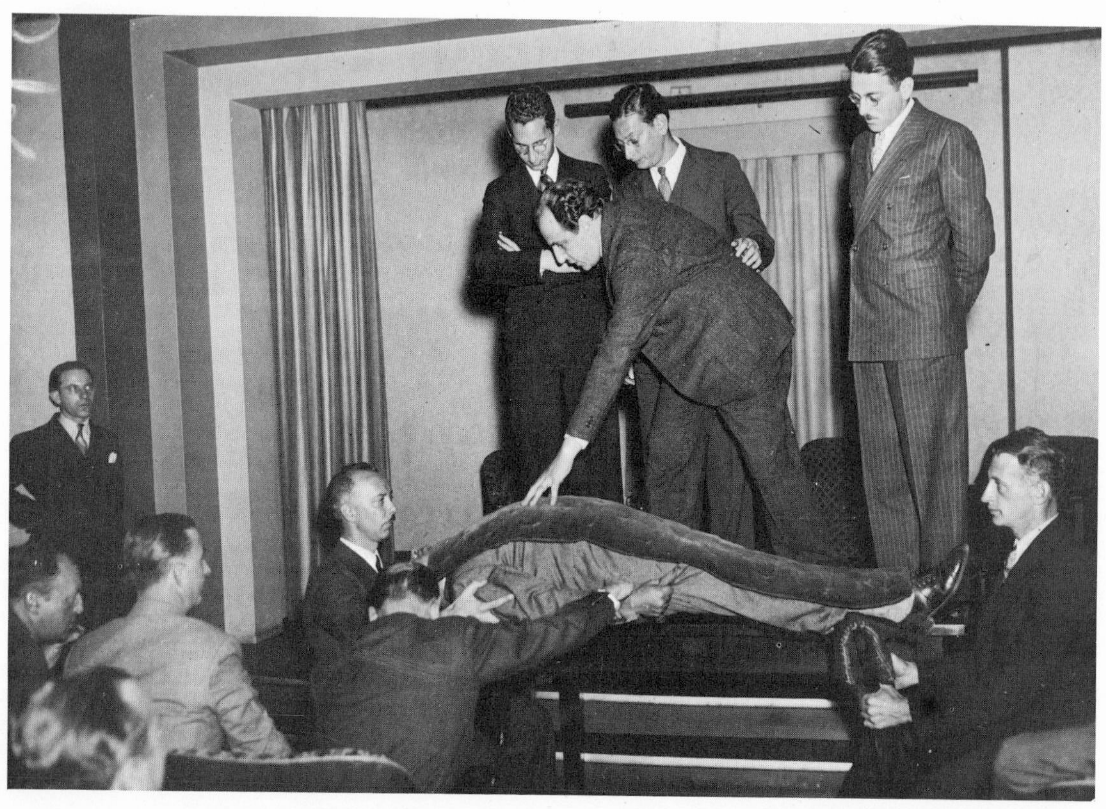

Former heavyweight champ Jack Dempsey verifies the accuracy with which Dunninger names the date on a coin.

Harry Blackstone and Dunninger inspect a pair of cuffs from Houdini's collection.

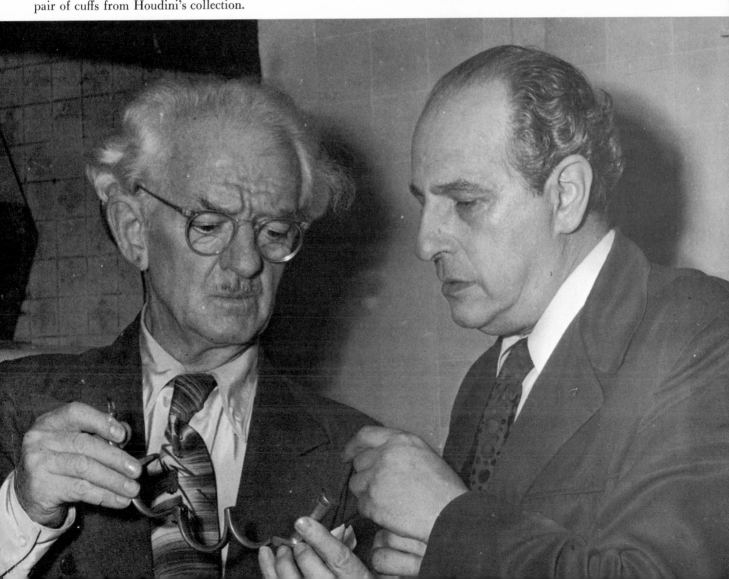

With Herbert Hoover and John Golden

With Gary Cooper

Cornel Wilde assisting the Dunningers in a telepathic experiment

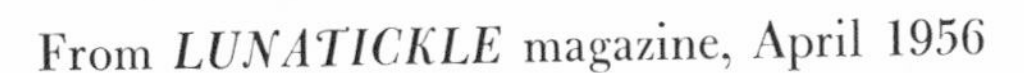

From *LUNATICKLE* magazine, April 1956

DUMMINGER

*MASTER MENTALIST**

Have you ever had the feeling that other people might easily be able to read your mind? .... That your deepest secrets were as clear to someone else as though they were written on your forehead? That all your hidden longings and desires were like an open book for the whole world to see?

In short, do you sometimes feel as if you were as transparent as glass? *Well, you're not,* so please sit down so that the rest of us can watch the DUMMINGER SHOW!

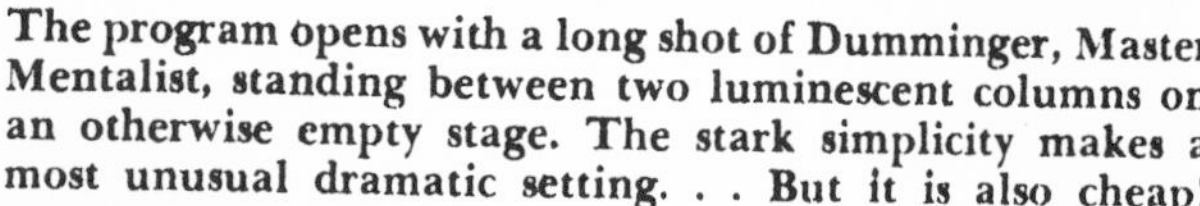

The program opens with a long shot of Dumminger, Master Mentalist, standing between two luminescent columns on an otherwise empty stage. The stark simplicity makes a most unusual dramatic setting. . . But it is also cheap!

Eerie music, supplied by the Eerie Mountain boys, is heard in the background. As the camera zooms in over the audience, the columns on either side of him light up, revealing the gaunt features of the Great Dumminger!

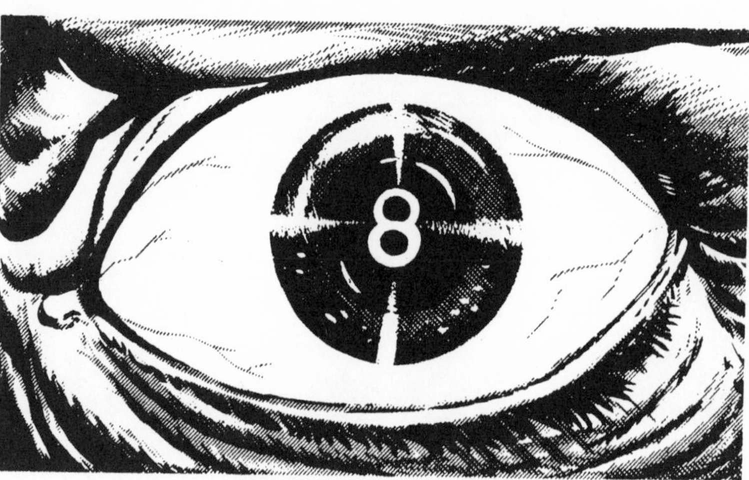

Then, as the music builds to a great, terrifying crescendo, we find ourselves even closer to the stark, mask-like face that stares intently at us. We are spellbound! Besides that, brother, we can't move! They glued all the seats!

Still closer comes the camera, until, with a horrendous crash of cymbals, nothing but a huge eyeball fills the screen! Can this unblinking orb actually read our minds? Can it probe our innermost thoughts? Can it, really?

The first guest of the evening, chosen by the studio audience to represent them, is brought out. He is Mr. Sam Bdurndurn, a patient at the Fliplid Mental Hospital, who has dared to challenge Dumminger to read his mind. This should be the slickest trick of the month, as it has not been established that Bdurndurn *has* a mind. A hush falls over the audience, partly because of the stark drama involved, but mostly because they're asleep!

DUMM: Do you give me your word that nothing has been arranged between us? Cross Your Heart! Scouts Honor? Would you swear it on a stack of Bibles? Bdurn: At these prices what jerk would refuse? I hate to take the dough.

Magnificent showman that he is, Dumminger orders a stack of Bibles wheeled out for his guest to swear on. And Mr. Bdurndurn really does swear when he realizes that the $10 bill Dumminger has slipped him is a counterfeit.

"YOU ARE THINKING OF A MAN'S NAME," says Dumminger, staring deep into Bdurndurn's eyes. "IT BEGINS WITH THE LETTER 'N'! . . . IT'S THE NAME OF A FAMOUS EMPEROR OF FRANCE. . . HE WAS DEFEATED AT WATERLOO! . . . THINK, NOW!

"AH, IT'S COMING IN STRONGER NOW! . . . THE FAMOUS EMPEROR YOU ARE THINKING OF IS N-A-P. . . NAPTHALENE. . . NO? NAPOHANSIC? . . . NO? (The anxious stagehands try to lend Dumminger moral support, and active support, too! Just look!

The mentalist's face lights up as recognition of the famous name finally occurs. "AHA, I'M GETTING THOSE LETTERS CLEARER NOW!" he announces triumphantly. "THE EMPEROR YOU ARE THINKING OF, FRIENDS, IS NAPOLEON IDIOT! AM I RIGHT?"

Some people claim that Dumminger purposely misses at times for dramatic effect. Few members of the studio audience, however, have such a flair for showmanship, and prove it by not missing with a barrage of fresh garbage. It is an audience participation show . . . as advertised!

At this point, Bob Moron, the announcer, gives a short, twelve minute demonstration of Hazel Botchup Lipstick, showing how, despite vigorous rubbing with steel-wool and coarse sandpaper, All-day Lipstick does stay on!

And here is the proof! Although the beautiful model's face, from her nose down, has been worn to the bridgework, her Hazel Botchup Lipstick is as good as new. After plastic surgery, she can put it back on! It is amazing!

So much for the commercial. And now, back to that part of the program in which Dumminger attempts to receive mental projections from the studio audience. We find him seated in the center of the bare stage like a great brooding Hamlet. His big eyes are half-closed, his fingers against throbbing temples, every nerve in his body straining to receive telepathic messages from his viewers. It is a real strainy night for Dumminger!

Meanwhile, the camera does a slow pan over the breathless, studio audience, proving to everybody that he is getting no outside help, and showing us that if Dumminger would OPEN his eyes, he'd get the messages much quicker. . . Especially since most of them are scrawled in letters over a foot high! Of course, he has to make believe he doesn't see them, and that is a masterful demonstration in itself, and adds materially to the socko impact.

Through some mystic, clairvoyant power, Dumminger is receiving a strong thought transference. The veins in his head bulge out and pulsate. "I'M GETTING THE NUMBER!" he announces solemnly, "IT IS A LONG, LONG NUMBER. . . WAIT, I'M—I'M GETTING CLOSER! . .

"I GET THE FIGURES 5-3-8-1-1-6! DO THEY MEAN ANYTHING TO ANYONE HERE?" he asks. (No response from the audience). Dumminger repeats the digits. "I'M GETTING THE NUMBER 538116! TELL ME, IS IT CORRECT? . . . WILL SOMEBODY TELL ME?"

"THAT IS ABSOLUTELY CORRECT! YOU'RE GETTING THE NUMBER 538116, BELIEVE ME!" announces Detective Reed Hardly of the Racket Squad, as he walks on stage from the wings. "YOU'RE UNDER ARREST FOR WITCHCRAFT, ALSO NECROMANCY. . . AND YOU'RE ALSO CHARGED WITH EXORCISING IN PUBLIC, AND YOU'RE WANTED FOR PEDDLING EVIL SPIRITS WITHOUT A LICENSE!" This sock finale sends the audience wild, but it makes Dumminger wilder, for this was not part of the act!

NOTE:

As all fans of the program know, Dumminger has posted a standing offer of $10,000 in cash (plus a one-way ticket to Zanzibar) payable to any viewer who can expose his mind-reading methods, and make it stick!

The editors of the MORONS' HOME JOURNAL would like nothing better than to have one of their readers come up with the secret and win that big money, especially if he would split it with them.

For that reason we are publishing, for the first time in any magazine, SIX LOGICAL POSSIBILITIES as to how Dumminger performs his amazing feats, and any one of these, with further research, might lead to the valuable prize money. Members of the staff of LUNATICKLE, lay off!

Here are the logical POSSIBILITIES:

1. **THE GUY CHEATS!**
2. **ALL DUMMINGER'S GUESTS ARE RELATIVES.**
3. **DUMMINGER IS REALLY A MARTIAN, WHERE TELEPATHY IS THE ONLY MEANS OF COMMUNICATION.**
4. **MASS HYPNOSIS**
5. **HE HAS AS HIS GUESTS, ONLY PEOPLE WITH GLASS HEADS.**
6. **THERE IS NO SUCH PERSON AS DUMMINGER, AND YOU'RE IMAGINING THE WHOLE THING!**

GOOD LUCK!

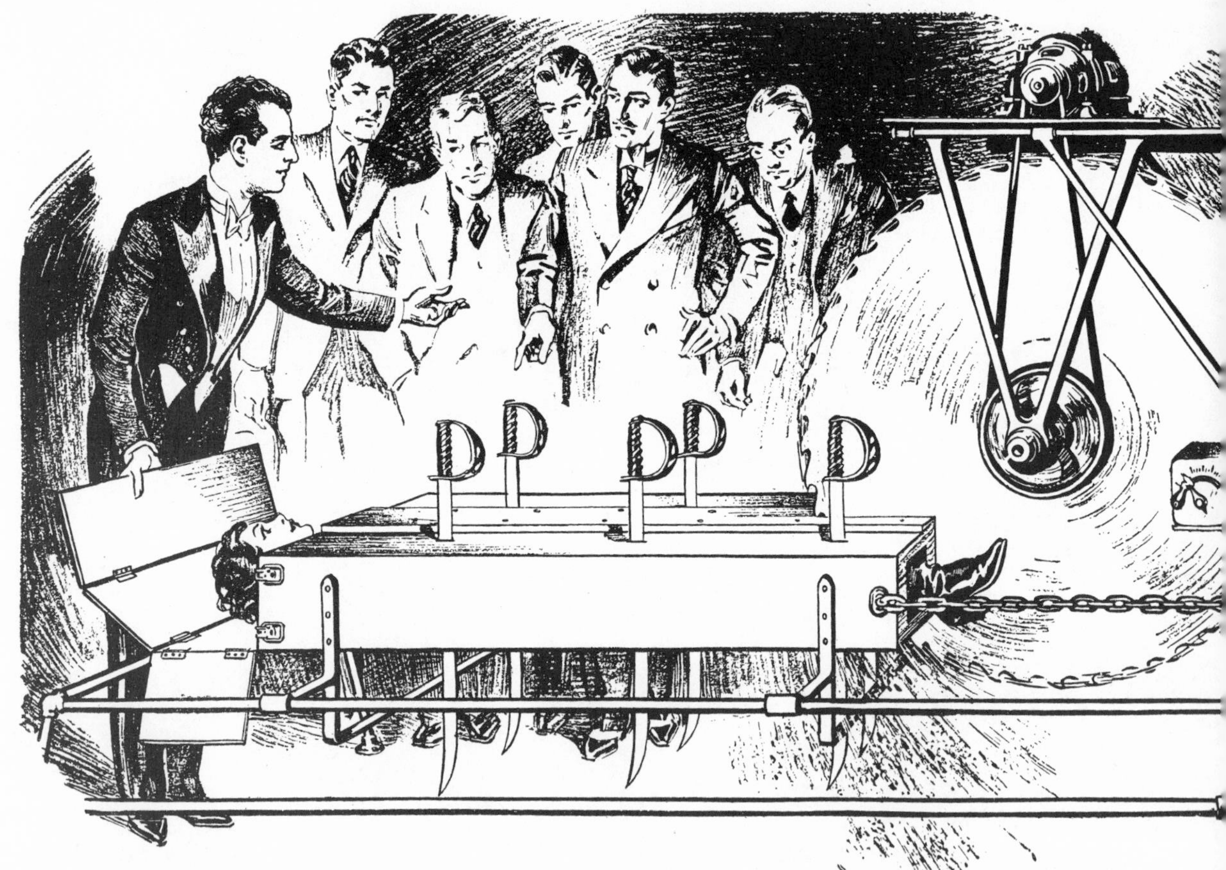

DUNNINGER'S *Sensational* Buzz-Saw Illusion

During Dunninger's travels, with his own two and one-half hour mystery show, touring both this country and abroad, the feature illusion was known as the *Buzz-Saw Illusion,* which not only created a sensation wherever presented, but has baffled the most learned minds of the entire world. Many explanations were offered, but up to date not one possible solution of the actual *modus operandi* of this startling mystery, which was created by Dunninger, has been forthcoming.

Mr. Dunninger's original idea was to exhibit this illusion on the vaudeville stage, but owing to the fact that this stupendous sensation carries so much necessary apparatus, machinery and a corps of trained assistants, the illusion would be too costly a proposition to present on the vaudeville stage today. With a full evening's performance it was quite a different matter.

The effect, in brief, of the Dunninger Buzz-Saw Illusion is as follows: A lady is apparently placed under hypnotic control, then lifted by two assistants and put into a box just large enough to hold her. Her feet are put through two circular holes at bottom of the box where they remain in full view throughout the experiment. Her wrists are placed under suitable steel bands on each side of the box and shackled in position by members of the audience, who are asked upon the stage to act as a committee and to see that everything is done in a fair and aboveboard manner. The locks used to hold the wrist bands may be brought upon the stage by anyone in the audience. These locks may be of any type desired.

The box, containing the lady, is now lifted on a skeleton track arrangement (see illustration), and two chains are

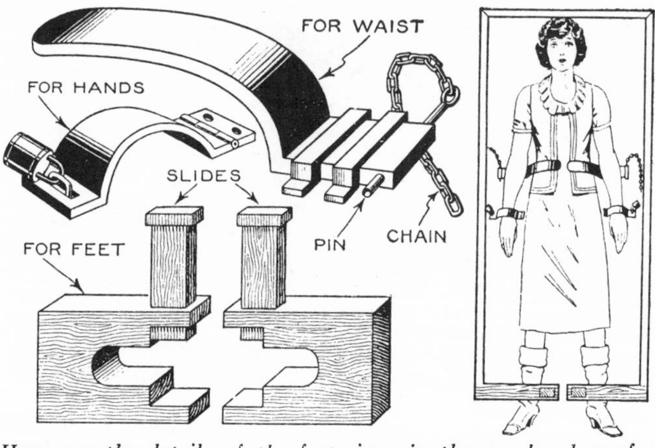

Here are the details of the fastenings in the wooden box of the illusion.

affixed to the box which are wound up on to a large drum manipulated by two assistants.

The girl being thus helplessly fastened in the box, it seems utterly impossible for her to move about, let alone make her escape.

Next, a number of swords are passed to committeemen and examined, then taken by the performer and thrust through the box from top to bottom. The swords enter the box at the top and project quite a bit outside of the bottom, proving conclusively that the swords have entered and passed completely through the box and apparently through the young lady.

Attention is now called to the buzz-saw, which stands on a specially built platform and skeleton stand contrivance. The saw is rotated by a powerful motor. The saw is put in operation and at the same time assistants, operating the drum slowly, set the same into motion and to the surprise, horror and mystification of the entire audience, the box containing the lady is seen, slowly but surely, inch by inch, to approach the whirling circular saw.

At last the box comes in contact with the buzzing saw and as the box continues to slowly slide along the skeleton tracks of the platform, the saw whirls its way, buzzing loudly through the box. When the box is in the position indicated in the diagram, the slaves are ordered to stop while the magician closes the top of the box covering the girl's head completely. Then the command to proceed is again given. The box is now completely sawed in half lengthwise . . . a feat never before, in the annals of magical history, accomplished by any magician the world has ever known!

The box is then pushed back to its former position, after committeemen make a thorough examination, proving to their own as well as the audiences' satisfaction that the box is completely sawed through; the box is then opened, the lady is freed of her manacles, brought out of her hypnotic trance by the performer and she trips daintily to the footlights to take her bow.

WHEN the casket is closed, the lady releases her hands by contracting her muscles and sliding her hands out of the shackles, which are sufficiently large. Her feet are withdrawn from the boots which have been stiffened with wire frames, to retain their form.

She now moves her body to the back section of the box, where she adjusts herself comfortably, aided by a trap cut in the back section, pushing outward and rendering additional room.

A loose board, hinged to the bottom of the box lined with metal, is pulled into position, and acts as a protecting shield. The girl adjusts her body so as to allow the three swords to pass her in entering their respective cavities.

With all arranged, the buzz saw can now pass through the box, with the girl comfortably protected.

Readjusting the trap, replacing the protection board, adjusting the shackles, and replacing her feet into the boots, everything is now ready for inspection at the finale.

The casket should be lined with black flannel or felt to make the working parts invisible and noiseless.

When the Fates Fooled

CHING LING FOO

And His Imitator—

CHUNG LING SOO

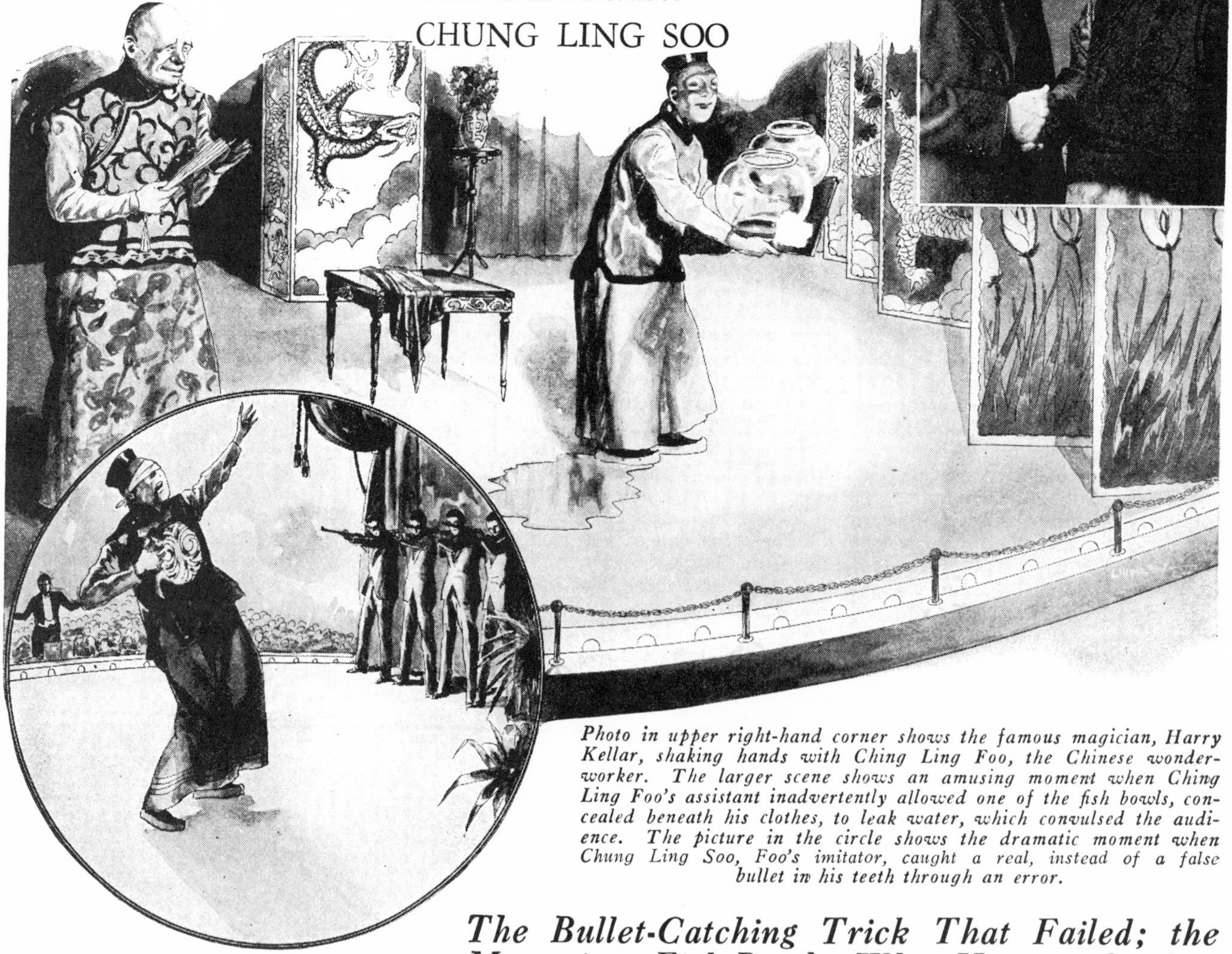

Photo in upper right-hand corner shows the famous magician, Harry Kellar, shaking hands with Ching Ling Foo, the Chinese wonder-worker. The larger scene shows an amusing moment when Ching Ling Foo's assistant inadvertently allowed one of the fish bowls, concealed beneath his clothes, to leak water, which convulsed the audience. The picture in the circle shows the dramatic moment when Chung Ling Soo, Foo's imitator, caught a real, instead of a false bullet in his teeth through an error.

The Bullet-Catching Trick That Failed; the Mysterious Fish Bowls; What Happened When Ching Ling Foo Challenged Chung Ling Soo

ALADDIN rubbed the wonderful lamp he discovered and every wish he made was fulfilled. Magicians and mentalists have discovered no lamp with these magical qualities, although many of us have, since the first disciple of the Magi made his appearance, sought in vain for an article of that type.

I know that if one delves back into the history of the lives of magic men, one is sure to find, not a collection of stories unfolding the sensational rise to success, fame and prosperity of magicians, but a sordid tale of trials and tribulations, heartaches and a persistent battle for supremacy.

Kellar, Devant, Ching Ling Foo, Houdini, De Bierre and many others, including the great Herrmann, fought for their places in the hall of magical fame, step by step, battling obstacles that never find their way into the paths of leaders in other vocations.

Take, for instance, the Chinese wonder-worker, *Ching Ling Foo.* For years this master among Chinese magicians appeared only in his own country and various parts of Europe. His share of the troubles and trials besetting the magic man were indeed many. But he gritted his teeth and in true Chinese fashion battled onward.

A. Frank Jones, who for years was the general booking manager for the Percy Williams circuit of theatres and for a long period associated with the world-famous Hammerstein's Victoria, brought Ching Ling Foo to America.

Mr. Jones was sent to Europe many times a season by the late impresario, Oscar Hammerstein, to seek out novelty acts that would, with the proper advertising and publicity campaigns, become sensations in this country. Foo and his troupe of orientals left their

Ching Ling Foo was fooled by Harry Kellar's "talking skull," and threw it down.

native shores and came here where they appeared for many weeks as the feature attraction on the Victoria bills. Always a real performer, showman and second to none as a modern miracle man, Foo became an overnight vaudeville sensation.

The troupe of fifteen experienced conjurers that Ching Ling Foo headed, startled even the host of American professional magicians and electrified our theatregoing public from the very beginning.

Chinese magic, seldom seen here, at once "caught on" and the clever Chinaman continued to work hard and create new effects that made the country ring with his name. Naturally there sprung up a number of "Chinese" illusionists, but they were considered by the booking men as just another space filler on a vaudeville bill.

Knowing from past experience that it always pays to be original, Foo toured the country with his company, raking in the golden shekels he had dreamed about in the days when he played before his own countrymen and the European audiences.

Ching Ling Foo's specialty was the production from *empty,* beautifully painted and embroidered shawls and flouards various sized glass bowls contained live goldfish. After convincing his spectators that he had nothing concealed about his person, Foo would turn a complete somersault and immediately after, produce a large bowl containing water and goldfish. This effect alone used to bring forth great applause.

The old saying has it—"be it ever so humble there is no place like home," and Foo longed for the rice-fields of his Flowery Kingdom. Soon the plaudits of his audiences held but little charm; his work was mechanically done. He longed to return to his native land.

Ching Ling Foo, with his company, returned to their homeland, carrying with him untold wealth. But as he once explained to his friend Harry Kellar, he was not unappreciative of the manner in which the American theatre-goers welcomed him.

About this time, in England, another "Chinese" conjurer made his début. Immediately this mysterious newcomer who was known under the stage *nom de plume* as Chung Ling Soo, in his act outshone the originator of that line of Chinese magic. For sometime, even in magical circles, much speculation was in the wind as to just who this mysterious Chung Ling Soo was.

Time went on and English theatre-goers showered this superior magician from the Flowery Kingdom with applause and filled his coffers with golden coins. Gradually it leaked out through unknown sources that the Chinaman who was startling England was an American, well-versed in the art of make-up. Finally it became whispered in inner channels that Chung Ling Soo was none other than William G. Robinson, a clever illusionist and character actor from Yankeeland. Soo's getup and the make-up of his assistants was as near perfection as possible. Robinson even went so far as to allow himself to be interviewed, through an interpreter, by members of the British Press. His London home was fitted up in true Oriental manner with hanging lamps, rich Chinese tapestries, and whenever the gentlemen of the press were visiting him, the pseudo-Chinaman received them in this intriguing Poppyland setting.

A humorous tale is related of Chung Ling Soo in which he was being interviewed by several reporters. "Do you like this country?" asked one of the scribes. The real Chinese interpreter, who was an acrobat and trusted assistant of Soo's, made answer, "I do. They are kind, generous and know as much as I do of my magic art."

"Have you ever been to America?" queried the other representative of the Fourth Estate.

"No," the interpreter translated, "but in my dreams I see large buildings and much water. And standing in a bay I see a large statue with one hand upraised holding the torch of light, lighting the way to freedom."

"Do you expect to return to America?" asked the skeptical newspaperman.

"How can one return to a place one has never been?" fenced the inimitable Billy Robinson, through the interpreter.

Several times during the engagement in England, Soo was invited by wealthy Chinese residents to attend social functions. Knowing full well the outcome of accepting any of these the psuedo-Chinaman refused under the excuse of pressing work and preparation of new effects but always had the faithful assistant see those who wished to interview him first.

The original Ching Ling Foo soon grew tired of the life of a Chinese country squire and the lure of the footlights began to assert itself. Then came to him in his celestial homeland reports of another who not only adopted a portion of his name but who was astounding audiences with many of his feature tricks.

Oriental brains began working. Foo issued a challenge to Soo. In 1905 during the month of January, Soo took up the "hat in the ring" edict and presented himself in the offices of an English newspaper to meet and outskill the skilled Foo. Robinson, alias Chung Ling Soo, had no other alternative. For an hour or more he entertained the news clan with magical tricks, awaiting the arrival of Ching Ling Foo, but the fates and the keen Oriental mind decided differently.

On the following day the newspaper office received a letter from the original Ching Ling Foo, announcing that he (Foo) would meet and take up the challenge with Soo only upon the condition that Chung Ling Soo appear before the Chinese Consul in London, and prove his claim to being a real Chinaman. This naturally never took place and was soon forgotten by the readers of the papers. They had seen Soo and voted him the cleverest of Chinese wonder workers and that was enough.

Billy Robinson was a friend of all who intimately knew him. He was an ingenious inventor and a skilled prestidigitator. He was a make-up artist of remarkable ability and an actor to his fingertips.

I still have and value very highly a fishing pole trick he presented me with while I was in England. This is one of the two tricks that won him fame.

The other was the illusion he created when allowing several soldiers to fire rifles at him and he would catch a marked bullet between his teeth. This trick startled all who witnessed it and finally was the cause of his death. Through some carelessness on the part of one of his assistants the faked bullets or cartridges that went into the guns and were fired at him, one of these was switched for a real bullet. That night, standing bravely before the firing squad, Billy smiled in his inimitable way and the rifles were fired. Robinson swayed a moment and then collapsed to the stage. The curtain was hastily rung down but when medical aid reached this sterling performer Chung Ling Soo was no more.

And so another master magician passed over the border to the land from where there is no return.

* * *

During one of Ching Ling Foo's performances he had to call on an assistant not familiar with the workings of a certain production trick, in which the conjurer holds a cloth before a tray, and when the covering is whisked away two large bowls, filled almost to the brim with water, in which goldfish merrily swim about, stand on the tray. This trick was worked by the assistant who had the bowls hung from each side of his vest under his flowing outer garment. The bowls are covered with tight-fitting caps which are taken off quickly as the bowls are placed upon the tray by the assistant under cover of the cloth. This assistant foolishly began to fumble with the water-proof cap on one of the goldfish containers and the water in the bowl leaked down his wide trouser-leg. You can picture his predicament under such a trying condition. But the assistant was game and with true Oriental stolidness he stuck to his post until the production was made, and then slowly walked off the stage carrying the tray and bowls with a stream of water flowing, which the strong lights made more noticeable than it otherwise would be. The audience howled their glee and stern Ching Ling Foo had to turn his back, for things of a humorous turn were very much enjoyed by this Celestial wonder worker.

The writer has a very interesting letter in his possession, sent to him some years ago by the late Harry Kellar, which describes a rather interesting and amusing episode that Kellar experienced with Ching Ling Foo. Foo, at the time, was visiting the aged magician, at his home in Los Angeles. Kellar had equipped his apartment with the necessary electrical wiring, whereby he would operate what was known as a talking skull. An induction coil, and a transmitter concealed in this papier maché skull, would produce voices, which in reality were those of an assistant in another room, speaking into a wireless telephone. For this occasion, Kellar had a Chinaman concealed in another room, who spoke through this apparatus, when Ching Ling Foo was listening in. So uncanny was the instance to Foo, that he turned white when the spook of some departed Chinese soul began conversing with him. In fear, he dropped the skull, and started for the door. Dropping the apparatus put the mechanism quite out of order, but this factor did not upset Kellar, as he writes that the laugh was worth it.

When Fate Fooled The Great Leon

The Great Leon, who perfected the Death Ray Gun illusion. The effect is shooting a girl through a solid steel plate.

AN insurance policy of $25,000 would bring exclamations of delight to any live-wire insurance agent: yet Miss Petite, twenty-five, who never knew a sick day in her life, was refused a policy for that amount!

And all because, as the assistant of a magical entertainer, she is fired two and three times a day from the muzzle of a large cannon through a steel plate into a net.

Hart and Enbank, 100 William Street, New York City, were the insurance agents who had to turn down what would be considered a desirable bit of business.

The illusion, one of the most sensational on the stage today, is owned and presented by the Great Leon, a magician and illusionist of considerable renown.

The effect of the illusion follows:

A smiling young miss is placed in a loaded cannon. A large sheet of examined steel is mounted in a frame directly in front of the muzzle. The cannon is fired; the report is extremely loud. The projectile is seen to penetrate the plate and pass entirely through. The young lady is assisted from the net and the steel plate is freely shown to the spectators and found to be quite intact.

Spirit mediums have time and again claimed that it is a form of spirit disintegration and materialization — in other words, that the body is transported by supernatural means from the cannon into the net, through the steel plate! As a matter of fact, the methods used are simple.

It required many years of scientific research, planning and working of several master magical mechanicians to perfect this startling and convincing magical feature presentation.

Miss Lillian White, who is shot through a steel plate three times a day.

During the experimentation several who were tried out as assistants were injured. Advertisements were inserted in newspapers requesting the services of trustworthy assistants, with the bait of bonuses for the right parties. Quite a number applied, but when Leon or his mechanicians explained what the duties of the assistant would be, all seemed to remember engagements elsewhere. To the brave came the thoughts of another day and its pleasures, so on their respective ways they went.

As there was no one forthcoming, and as Leon knew whoever did act the part of the human projectile would be endangering his life, he took the duties of assistant on himself. One day things went wrong, the Goddess of Luck winked a wicked eye, and the Leon woke up in the French hospital.

Finally things were straightened out by a well-known mechanician. For some weeks the illusion was presented before large audiences in the leading big-time vaudeville theaters of the country; but bad luck was to have its fling once more.

One evening an assistant loaded the cannon with a supply of gunpowder, without apprising the man who was assigned to this task. The "official loader" charged the cannon with another round or supply of gunpowder. When the gun was touched off the lady in the steel shell escaped injury by some miraculous chance, but the scenery was shot to pieces and a fire was averted only through the quick work of several of the actors on the bill.

More experiments followed. The cannon was rebuilt. Two years passed by. Constant experimentation brought its reward. The act was perfected and made harmless to the assistant who acted the rôle of projectile.

Another illusion the Great Leon has been associated with is the Fire and Water sensation. In this illusion a lady is presumably burned at the stake, a shot is fired and she makes her appearance in a glass case, filled with water. She steps out of this case dripping wet. Several mishaps, when fate proved all unkind took place in various theatres where Leon was appearing. One night the lady didn't make her getaway quickly enough from beneath the shroud-like robe and the flames shot up and severely burned her. One or two other assistants received second and third degree burns when attempting this startling effect. But Leon has now perfected this illusion so that but little danger of injury to the assistants is possible.

An experience my friend La Vellma had some years ago is interesting. In each town La Vellma hired a "plant" fellow, who, for so much per show, would come up on the stage when invited by the entertainer and act natural, thereby getting more out of this natural type of clowning than if he attempted to be funny. The town in question was one of those places where everybody knows the town loafer. This was the fellow La Vellma picked. Instructing him what to do he gave the fellow a dollar and told him to hand that to him when he asked him for a loan of a bill during the performance.

The curtain rose on the magician's act and during the course of events everything was going along smoothly and the crowd out front was very appreciative; the fellow was invited to step upon the stage and assist in the following experiment. Up stepped the town clown and upon being recognized by the spectators was given a big hand. Awkwardly bowing his thanks the fellow was asked by La Vellma for the loan of a dollar. This got another big laugh from the spectators. Fishing down in his pocket the clown handed the performer thirty-five cents. "But I asked for the loan of a dollar," said the master of legerdemain. Then in a more serious voice, "What did you do with the dollar bill I gave you this morning?"

Again a laugh from the amused audience, but the biggest laugh of all was yet to come when the loon replied, "That's all I have left of it. I was hungry and I bought some dinner!"

When the Fates Fooled Dunninger

Tricksters Who Constantly Toy With Fate Sometimes Find That Fate Plays Pranks on Them. In This Story by Dunninger About His Own Experiences, Dunninger Leaves the Only Two Tools Necessary for Opening a Safe From the Inside, a Screw-driver and a Flashlight, in His Coat Pocket; Then Has Himself Locked in the Safe Without His Coat. With the Supply of Oxygen Failing . . . Read What Happens.

TO anyone who wishes to succeed as a magician I give the same advice . . . practice and study, then practice again. Some take the advice; others do not. For the fact remains that to reach the top in magic, mind reading or kindred arts, one must give the best there is in him. He must aim to be original, if not in the experiments selected, at least in the presentation of them. If you are a patter magician, be sure of the type of patter you use. Don't rewrite or copy the other fellow's material. Have patter especially written around your tricks. It costs very little proportionately, and the results are well worth the expense. But to get to my experiences.

Many years ago I purchased the entire stock of magic from the Crest Trading Company and circulated extensively throughout the world. For months I was deluged with orders for magical apparatus and tricks. I was surprised at the vast number of people interested in magic. I employed quite a staff filling and mailing out orders. Among the orders received were some that afforded me many laughs.

For instance, one fellow in South America sent in an order for what is known to magicians as a pigeon pan. The effect in brief to an audience is a highly nickeled pan, something on the order of a chafing dish, placed on a table into which several eggs are broken. These are then seasoned with salt and pepper. These ingredients are mixed together and a cover placed on the pan. A few magic words, or a revolver is fired, and when the cover of the pan is removed, live pigeons fly out of it.

The effect is startling and sure-fire. Well, to get back to my story . . . the fellow who ordered it immediately wrote me that he received the pan and was pleased with it, but the pigeons had not, as yet, arrived. Naturally, no pigeons are included with the trick, as a pair can easily be procured anywhere. Feeling in a jesting mood, I answered the would-be magician's letter and told him that I had sent the pigeons out to him through my window, with his name and address tied around their necks, but due to the storms, perhaps, the pigeons had sought shelter and would eventually arrive. Some weeks later the fellow wrote back informing me that although he had slept for several weeks with his windows wide open the pigeons hadn't put in their appearance.

Another order came for a production bowl to produce candy. The customer wrote that he only wanted a bowl that would produce, by magical means, creamed chocolates, as his sweetheart preferred that kind of candy. He also wanted to know if I would guarantee the quality of the candy the bowl would magically produce!

The levitation of a woman in midair was also advertised in my list and a South American, who had fallen in love with the Goddess of Magic, sent an international money order for the effect, explaining that when I sent the apparatus I should be sure to send along a blonde woman with the outfit because he claimed that blondes were more to the liking of the people of his country!

Just before I closed out the entire stock I received a long letter from a woman who wrote she was poor but honest, and although she couldn't afford to purchase, for cash, a money-catching wand which I had advertised, she would send me letters of reference if I sent her the wand and she would in return forward me one-half of all the money she could catch. She also asked how many half dollars she would be able to catch in a week or two! Imagine that!

While doing handcuff escapes on the stage, I once issued my customary challenge to police officers to bring their own cuffs, from which I would release myself upon the stage. As I spoke I noticed a man seated in the front row dropping buckshot into the locks of his pair of handcuffs. It is impossible for anyone to free himself from handcuffs that have been doctored with buckshot. Saying nothing, I invited a committee upon the stage to examine the cuffs and assist in manacling me. Up stepped the wise guy carrying his handcuffs. Watching my chance, I took the handcuffs from him and grasping his wrist, snapped a cuff onto his wrist, pressing the side catch. Then I said, "I want to have the ladies and gentlemen out there see how easy it is for you to open those cuffs of yours with the key!"

Picture my predicament if I hadn't by sheer luck glanced in his direction when I first made my entrance on the stage!

I could unfold a thousand and one tales of the mishaps, the laughs and the comical situations that have arisen during my various entertainments before celebrities and in the homes of the élite. After showing a few magical tricks to the Prince of Wales he said to me, "Say, Dunninger, when you come over to England I want you to meet the folks and show them a few of those tricks, will you?"

When the entertainer least expects it, drama creeps into his work. I will never forget the thrill and fright I received one night that the people out front never suspected. Even my own assistants didn't know at the time what a narrow escape I had from being suffocated to death.

It came about in this manner. . . . I used to feature a thrilling strait-jacket release and the escape from a large safe, borrowed from the leading safe dealer in whatever town I was playing. One night I would do the safe trick, the next the strait-jacket release.

This night I stepped out on the stage and announced I would endeavor to make my escape from the safe. In this trick I used a searchlight so as to see the darkness of the safe in order to operate the tumblers from within. It perhaps isn't generally known, but tumblers in a safe can be operated from the inside by anyone understanding their workings by removing the plates after taking out the screws which hold them in place.

On the heels of the announcement a voice in the audience rang out: "I demand that you, Dunninger, escape or make an attempt to escape from this strait-jacket which I brought from the Such-and-Such asylum!"

"But, my dear sir, tonight I have scheduled my escape from this safe," I announced to the challenger as I pointed to the large safe which stood on the stage.

"Makes no difference. I insist on the strait-jacket!" called the man in the audience.

"If you insist, sir, I shall leave it to the audience, whom I am here to please." I expected the audience to pass his challenge up—but they yelled that I should do both the strait-jacket escape and the safe release! So I had to do them.

I requested the challenger to step upon the stage with his restraint jacket—one used only on the most violently insane unfortunates.

Stripping off my coat, in the pockets of which were my small trusty screw-driver and searchlight, I tossed the coat over a chair. During the process of being manhandled and buckled into the restraint apparatus, I forgot all about it.

Officers recruited from the audience who assisted in the operations were experts in their line. I was handled none too gently, and the spectators out front seemed to sense this, for hisses greeted the efforts of the strong-arms.

When I was bound in approved asylum style I requested the committeemen to stand to one side. In full view I managed to make my escape from that murderous restraint jacket.

A thunderous volume of applause greeted my release and for a few moments I stood, nearly exhausted, bowing my thanks to the audience for their generous applause.

When I had regained my breath, I was ready to try the safe trick. The safe was opened, I stepped into it, and it was quickly locked. I knew my assistants were wheeling my cabinet around the safe to cover my escape methods from prying eyes. I was ready to work. I placed my hands in my pockets . . . pockets that were not there! Then I remembered.

My coat was outside on a chair—and I had neither screw-driver nor search-lamp!

Here I was in total darkness, with barely enough room to move, and without the necessary means of making my escape!

And they say the work of an escape artist is a sinecure!

Fumbling as best I could with the plates over the tumblers . . . with the oxygen rapidly being used up . . . with no means of attracting or signaling my assistants . . . I was gradually enveloped in a panic! Beads of perspiration dripped from my forehead striking my cold, nervous hands like drops of melted lead. . . . I fought the panic and fear that were slowly getting the best of me.

Searching in the back pocket of my trousers I got out my key-ring. The gods were with me! I had a sort of screw-driver fashioned some time before with a file, at the end of a long skeleton key . . . in my panic I had entirely forgotten it.

Now I set to work again on the plate covering the tumblers of the safe. My head seemed ready to burst . . . my tongue was parched . . . my head splitting . . . I tore the collar from my dress shirt . . . then the neck . . . I must continue to breathe . . . finally the tumblers clicked into place. . . . I was free . . . free!

I had just enough strength left to push open that door . . . the sounds of the orchestra sounded faintly in my ears . . . I staggered forward . . . fell . . . then darkness!

When I came to, I was seated in a chair back stage. A doctor was holding a bottle of smelling salts to my nostrils. My assistants and the stage crew were standing about, with faces as white as sheets.

"Narrow escape that!" volunteered the physician.

"Dunninger, we were afraid you were gone!" my first assistant told me.

"The lamp and the screw-driver were in my coat——" I was too weak to talk.

"Yes. I found that out after they had locked you in," replied my assistant.

"That safe stuff is out from now on!" I managed to say.

Fervently I heard my man, who had been with me for several years, reply, "Amen!"

And never again, in the several years I continued to do escape stunts, did I include the escape from a borrowed safe!

Dunninger with Howard Thurston, the magician. At 36 the former's accomplishments already rival those of his older predecessors

Simple Parlor Magic

● IF you ask someone to balance a billiard ball on the top of another ball, he will probably refuse to try. When you do it, your task will be made easy if you secretly put a little pile of chalk on the top of the first ball, and rest the second ball on it. But, before you present the result to your audiences, blow away all superfluous chalk (Fig. 1)

Another catch is to support coins on nothing. To do this, take a small empty paper cigarette packet, and place a smooth round pencil in it. Rub the packet and pencil firmly up and down on some varnished woodwork. Release your hand cautiously, and the packet will adhere so firmly to the woodwork that often it may be filled completely with coins without falling (Fig. 2).

The experiment shown in Fig. 3 always amazes those who do not know the trick.

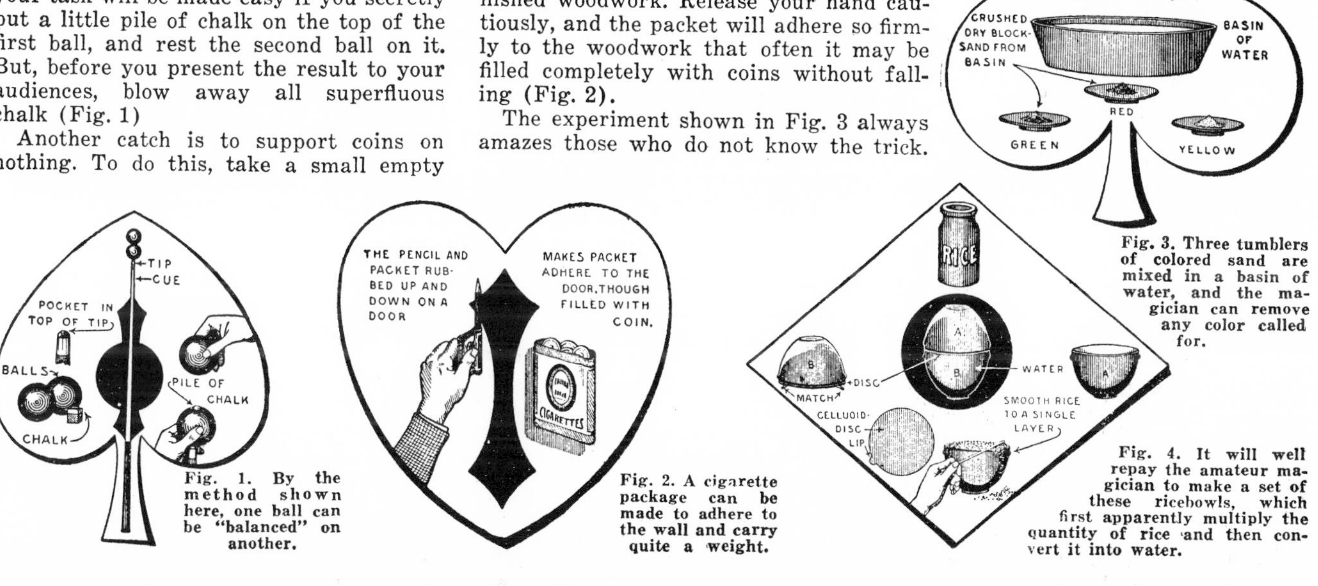

Fig. 3. Three tumblers of colored sand are mixed in a basin of water, and the magician can remove any color called for.

Fig. 1. By the method shown here, one ball can be "balanced" on another.

Fig. 2. A cigarette package can be made to adhere to the wall and carry quite a weight.

Fig. 4. It will well repay the amateur magician to make a set of these ricebowls, which first apparently multiply the quantity of rice and then convert it into water.

Obtain two small and similar china bowls. To a sheet of plate glass, secure some fine emery cloth; invert one bowl on the cloth and rub until you produce a flat edge. Cut a circle of clear celluloid to fit the outside diameter of the basin, leaving a lip as shown. Fill the bowl with water and cover it with the cardboard circle. The bowl may now be inverted without the water escaping. (Sometimes a bowl may be found that does not require grinding or, with care, the experiment may even be performed with a round edged rim.)

Fig. 5. The way to arrange a cigarette paper so that it will not burn.

Put three matches radially on a tray, to prevent the inverted bowl of water from making close contact with the tray. Then get a pound of rice in a jar and you are ready to start. Show empty bowl A. Then fill with rice. Without letting the cardboard disc be seen, cover bowl A with the inverted bowl B. Dramatically raise both bowls in the air and replace them on the tray, reversing their respective positions. Raise A and some rice pours onto the tray. Say that it has got damp and swollen. Level off the rice until a single grain layer *only* covers the cardboard. Cover B with A and raise the bowls again. As you replace on the tray this time, do not reverse them. As you uncover B, carry away with A the celluloid. Put A and the celluloid on the spilled rice on the tray, in an inverted position. Now pour the water from bowl to bowl several times; it looks more than it really is.

When done well, this item never fails to evoke surprise and applause.

Here is an item (Fig. 4) which was once popular. To prepare, get three handfuls of sand and dye each portion a different color. Fry each lot in tallow; in an ordinary frying pan, piece of tallow about the size of a walnut is required. Using matchbox drawers as molds, press some sand in each; in this way, make a number of blocks of each color. Put one block of each color in a tumbler. Fill up each tumbler with the *same* colored sand as the block already in position.

To perform—with a magician's flourish empty each tumbler into a basin of water; the blocks, being the same color as the sand in each case, will not be detected falling. Stir the mixed sand. Show your hand empty and then fish for any of the three colors that may be called for. When you find a block of the right color, as you bring your hand out, crush the block in your closed hand. You may then pour out the selected colored sand on a saucer. This will be *dry* (because of the tallow coating, of course). Repeat for the two remaining colors.

Here is a simple trick. Ask a friend to strike a safety match on the sole of his shoe. He will fail, but you will be able to do so if you have slightly moistened the striking side of a matchbox and rubbed it on your sole under the instep, thus transferring some of the igniting preparation. In the protected position indicated, the transferred preparation will last for quite some time. (A leather sole is best for this.)

Ask your friends this one: Can you put a cigarette paper in such a position that it cannot be burned? Do it this way. Wrap it round a tumbler tightly. A flame applied to the paper will then not burn it. (Fig. 5).
—*Armchair Science*

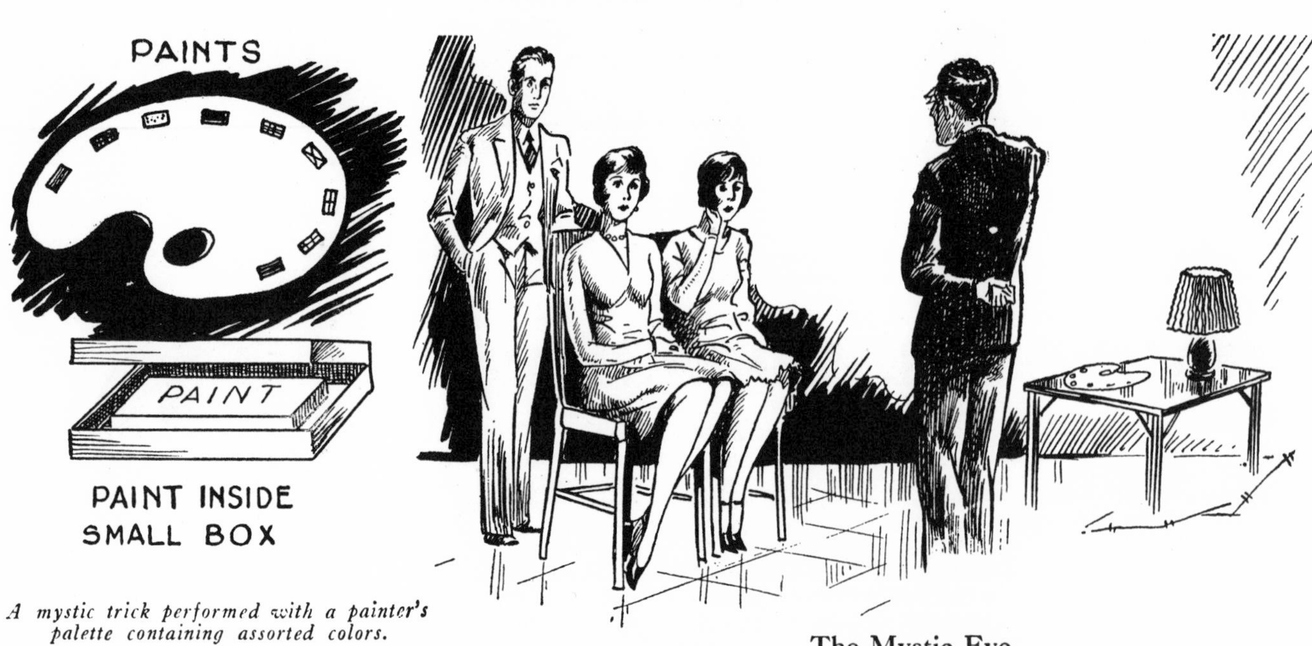

A mystic trick performed with a painter's palette containing assorted colors.

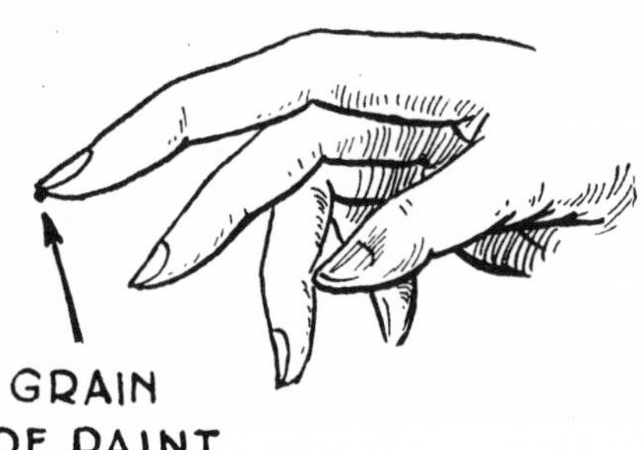

Above: How the magician gets a sample of the paint as he holds the box behind his back.

The Mystic Eye

THIS is a novel and effective thought-reading trick. A painter's palette, with a number of small squares of paints of assorted colors, is passed for inspection. A small nickel-plated box, slightly larger than the squares of paints, is likewise examined. As these articles are actually unprepared, rigid inspection is invited. During the wizard's absence from the room, one of the spectators is requested to place one of the paints into the box. Upon the magician's return, he is handed the box, which he holds behind his back in the one hand, while he raises his other hand to his head, to enact a picture of deep concentration. Shortly he calls the color of the paint concealed in the box.

Secret: In the act of holding the box behind his back, the wizard quickly opens it for a moment and secures a few grains of the paint beneath his finger-nail by scratching the nail across the surface of the square. In the act of raising his hand to his head, he thus has but to secretly observe the color beneath his nail.

MAGIC

The Floating Glass

A GLASS and a pitcher of milk is carried forward by the magician. The glass is filled with milk and a few mystic passes are made over it with one hand. The other hand then lets go off the glass which remains suspended in the air. The glass is now caused to float away from the performer's hands and again when he beckons it, it glides back to his fingers. During this mystic levitation, the magician removes a hoop which has been hanging around his neck and passes it around the glass. Secret: This is a variation of a trick originated by the author many years ago. As will be observed, the black silk thread passes through two holes in the glass, loops around the ear at one end and is held by an assistant at the other. By manipulating the thumbs of the hands over the thread, and by the concealed assistant raising and lowering the thread, the glass is caused to float in various directions. The hoop is handled as illustrated.

HARNESS ON CONFEDERATE

Powerful Spirits

THIS demonstration is excellent for an anti-spiritualist act. The magician directs attention to a strongly built large size kitchen table and invites a committee of five or ten to step up on the platform and examine the table. After it has been declared unprepared, one of the spectators is asked to sit on the tabletop and the rest are then requested to put their palms on the table and press down upon the same. A few mystic passes and the table floats into the air, even though every effort is made to hold it down. The secret: The magician has a confederate in the audience who is called upon the stage as a spectator. Both magician and confederate are equipped with a special harness (if the magician partakes in the lifting stunt), or if he moves away from the table, two confederates are supplied with the harnesses. The illustration makes

the type of harness clear. Note the plate which is pulled down in such a way that it comes under the table top and this serves as the means for lifting the table clear off the floor. The assistants need merely stoop a little, pull down the plate, and then lift.

Mesmerized Pencil

TO present this startling little pocket trick, the only essential paraphernalia is the attachment made for regular pencils to be used for turning the dials on a dial telephone, and a metal tube into which the pencil will loosely fit. Both of these pieces can be obtained in the average five and ten cent store or in a stationery store. Close inspection of the pencil, the metal dialing end and the tube, reveals no preparation. Holding the case in the left hand, the magician draws the pencil out of its holder with the right hand, the pencil and tube being supported horizontally. Suddenly releasing the pencil, it is found to quickly snap back into its holder as if drawn in by a powerful suction apparatus or by a rubber band. The pencil is again passed for examination, as is the holder, but the closest of inspection proves it to be devoid of any mechanism or arrangement. The secret: This trick is an exception inasmuch as the apparatus is exactly what it seems to be; namely, quite unprepared. The round ball, attached to the end of a pencil (commonly used for dialing a telephone) is held between the thumb and index finger. By squeezing these fingers together and sliding them slightly, enough force is produced to cause the pencil to snap back into the holder with such speed that the spectators actually believe a rubber band or a spring accomplishes the effect.

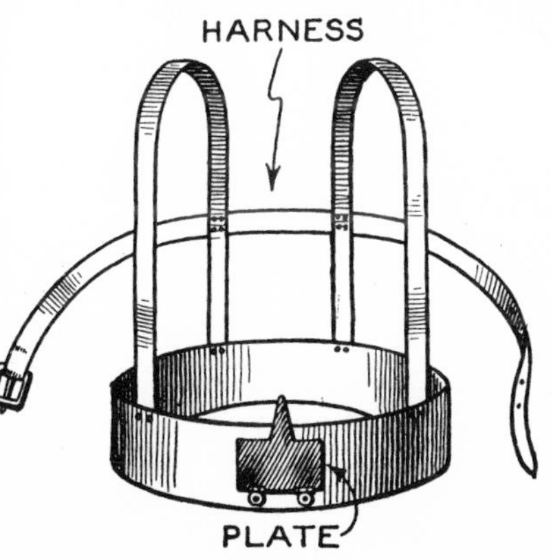

Telepathy De Luxe

THIS exceptional trick in thought transference can be presented as an impromptu demonstration, with absolutely no prearranged paraphernalia. The wizard explains that he can use a radio to demonstrate the possibility of broadcasting thoughts over the ether. The loud speaker is disconnected from the set and the earphones are attached. The assistant who is to partake in this demonstration is now led to another room, and after a committee has been chosen they impart a word and the name of a playing card to this assistant, who naturally is stationed at a fair distance from the performer. The committee return to the radio chamber, and after a few moments are amazed to find that the magician is in possession of the secret name or card.

Explanation:. Anyone who has experimented with radios knows that if an electric switch be turned on or off in another room a click or sound is distinctly heard. A code is prearranged and the trick is done.

Wand Vanish De Luxe

THE effect: The magician proves the wand that he has been using to be solid and apparently unprepared, by giving it a few violent raps upon atable top. Taking a sheet of newspaper which has been hanging across the back of a chair, he tears the paper in two and proceeds to wrap the wand snugly into one of the sections of the paper. Without any suspicious moves he nonchalantly tears this paper into small sections, the wand having completely disappeared.

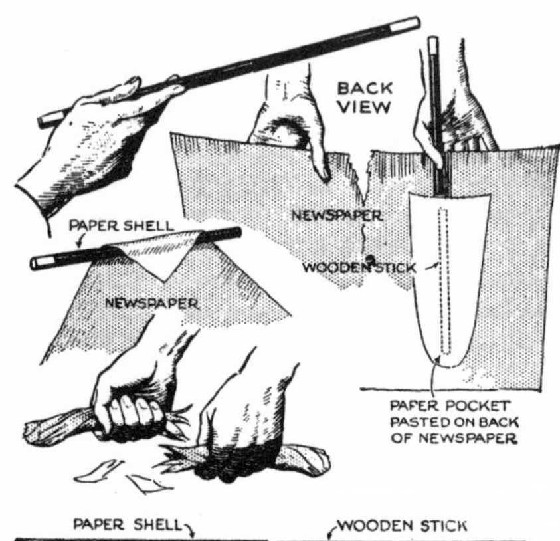

The secret: The wand consists of a wooden stick, concealed within a piece of paper tubing, which has been painted to represent the genuine article. In the act of tearing the newspaper in two, the solid stick slides from out the tube into a newspaper pocket which has been pasted in back of the paper. Thus, the paper tube which, to all appearances, is the solid wand, is rolled into the newspaper which is afterward torn to bits.

The Phantom Derby

THE magician enters a room, and for a moment shocks the ladies by neglecting to remove his hat. Seeming to be somewhat embarrassed, the wizard places his finger to his mouth, and blows upon it. Instantly, the derby leaps off the magician's head, flying into the air.

An examination of the hat is sure to be called for. The spectators, however, are greatly amazed to find the derby is entirely unprepared.

Secret: Two plain pins and a piece of elastic is all that is required. A pin is tied firmly to each end of the elastic. Stretching the elastic, the pins are driven directly opposite one another into the band of the hat. The derby is then placed upon the head, as illustrated. The hat should fit rather tightly. In the act of blowing the finger, which is merely a bit of by-play, the wizard has but to frown, thereby relaxing the muscles of the forehead, which produces sufficient slack to cause the hat to fly upward, and offthe conjurer's head.

All that remains to be done is to remove the pins and elastic secretly.

Enchanted Goblet

THE wizard brings forth a large, transparent glass goblet. This container is seen to be filled with milk.

The magician then borrows a handkerchief, which he throws over the goblet, and places it on a table. To the amazement of the spectators, the goblet is brimfull of wine when kerchief is removed.

The goblet is a specially prepared one, with hollow stem, and an inner glass lining. Some milk is poured in through the stem, while the glass is inverted. A cork prevents the milk from leaving. The inner lining is filled with wine, concealed from view by the milk in the outer shell. When covering the goblet with the handkerchief, the cork is secretly removed, and the forefinger pressed over the hole.

The glass is placed over a trap in the magician's table, the inside of which contains a tin cup, into which the milk freely flows, while the goblet is still covered.

In the usual straight jacket releases, much strenuous work must be done before the magician can liberate himself from the jacket. With this jacket a lace permits the jacket to expand, aiding freedom.

Improved Straight Jacket Release

THE magician who has heretofore favored the effect of liberating himself from the regulation straight jacket has, in all probability, eliminated it from his program, due to the strenuous manual labor which was necessary to effect his escape. In this improved trick, the straight jacket has an extra pleat sewed into the back, which is, of course, covered from view, by an outer and inner layer of cloth. This additional space is drawn together by means of a strong lace, as illustrated. The lace is held firmly in place by two small hooks, held to two rings, sewed upon the lower edge of the jacket. As the magician is strapped into the affair, his trained assistant secretly releases these laces, during the operation of adjusting the final strap between the conjurer's legs. As the wizard rolls about the floor, the jacket secretly expands, making it a simple matter to slip it over his head. The rest of the effect is carried out exactly as in the usual straight jacket release; namely, one arm is first forced over his head, and this is subsequently followed by the other arm.

Rapid Transit Dimes

THIS method of presenting an ever-popular effect will give the amateur wizard an opportunity of duplicating what is apparently the outcome of years of practice. Four dimes are made to disappear by any of the methods which a magician usually employs, or any of those described in previous articles of this series. On the table or on a tray, the spectator will find a group of unprepared oranges, any of which he may examine at will, and then present to the magician. The wizard cuts a gash into the fruit, then completely splits it. On opening the pieces, the dimes will be seen to have found their way into the interior. The secret lies in the construction of the knife, the sides of which are made of thin steel, and so arranged that they form a compartment for the holding of the dimes. The first part of the cut into the fruit is made in the ordinary way. After that, the knife is tipped upward, so as to permit the dimes to slide out of it, and distribute themselves about the cut.

In this effect any one of a group of oranges is selected by a member of the audience. This is examined to prove that it has not been tampered with. The magician then picks up a knife from the table, cuts into the fruit, which on being opened, reveals the coins.

Bran to Candy

THIS is a vast improvement over the old experiment of a somewhat similar effect. It will be remembered that in the old stunt the performer fills a goblet with bran, and empties it, to prove that the glass contains nothing but bran. This is done several times, after which the container, apparently full of bran, is covered with a metal cap which, on being removed, discloses the glass full of candy. In this modern version, instead of using a metal cover, a cylinder of paper is employed which, on being removed, is crushed up and thrown away. The effect is produced by the aid of a paper feke (instead of a metal one), made to fit the container. To this a thin layer of bran has been glued. This feke contains the candy and it is loaded into the glass goblet under pretext of filling it with bran from the box. The feke is removed with a newspaper cylinder, leaving the candy behind. The feke is then crushed in the newspaper and thrown away.

In this effect a goblet of bran is converted into one full of candy. A paper feke covered with bran which contains the candy, is employed. The feke is crushed in the newspaper cylinder and thrown away.

Amateur magicians often lose sight of the fact that to put over any trick well, whether for private or public performances, there is invariably required a good patter or "side talk." In many cases the change or pass in a certain trick is accomplished while the performer is speaking some such line as, "Now watch my hands closely; the hand is quicker than the eye." The audience watches sharply, but the trick or pass is made so skillfully, under the cover of some "camouflage" like the above, that they do not see how it is done.

Hindu Burial

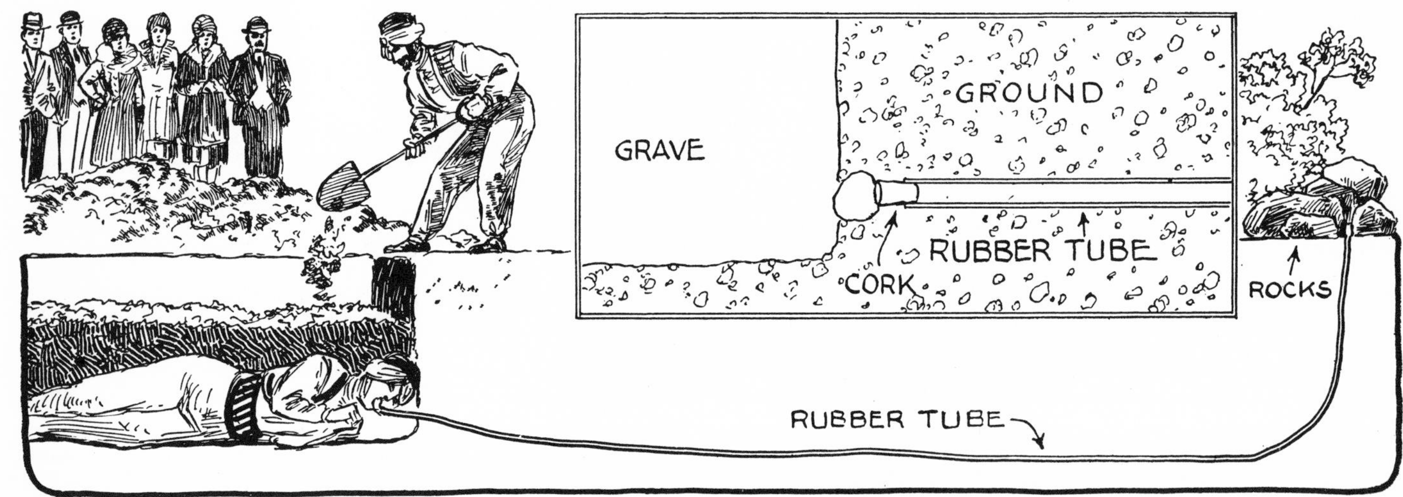

In this illustration we find a version of a "Hindu Burial." It will be observed that the grave although seemingly unprepared has been dug at a spot where the subject can easily get at a rubber hose leading through the ground and terminating in a pile of rocks some distance from the burial spot. He can breathe through this tube for several hours. It will be noticed that the end of the tube near the grave is corked and then covered by a small stone making it easy to locate the tube yet effectively concealing it from those who may be curious enough to examine the grave. There are, of course, other ways of performing this trick, but this is one of the simplest.

The Flying Coin

THE requirements for this trick consist of an unprepared glass tumbler, a paper cylinder which can be made up just before the trick is presented and a rather thick book. All of these articles are passed for inspection. When returned to the wizard he places the tumbler on the book and then covers this with the paper tube. He next asks someone for a half dollar which should be marked and then handed to the magician. The magician stands twenty to thirty feet away from the cylinder and invisibly tosses the coin into the glass. It is there heard to fall with a very distinct clink. The effect is accomplished by aid of a metal tube housing a spring and coinholder which when released tosses the coin upward and into the glass as indicated by the dotted lines.

In this effect a glass is placed on a book then covered with a cylinder and a coin previously vanished invisibly leaps into the glass.

The Haunted Cigarette Box

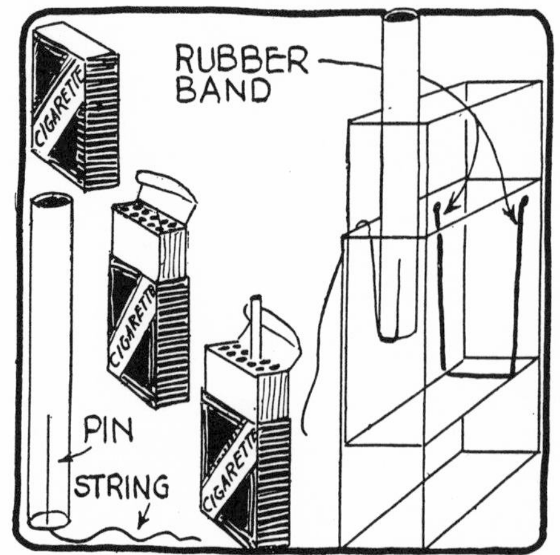

Here is a trick which anyone can prepare at practically a moments notice. The box arises automatically and after that a cigarette moves up from it.

THIS is an exceptionally good pocket trick, quite amazing in effect, and requires but very little preparation. A request for a cigarette is a rather common occurrence and with this in mind the magician has prepared beforehand for something bound to startle his spectator. In effect, the magician takes a pack of cigarettes from his pocket, makes some mysterious passes over the top, the box rises, opens, and a cigarette pushes its way out of the center. The only paraphernalia required is a rubber band, a piece of black thread and a pin. The rubber band is threaded through the outside cover of the cigarette box as indicated and one of the cigarettes is prepared with the thread and pin. Releasing pressure on the cover causes the contents to rise and pushing the box forward brings the cigarette out of the package.

The Mystic Envelope

THIS effect can be converted from one form of presentation to another. Either the card can be changed to an envelope or the envelope can be converted to a card. We will describe but one form of presentation. A deck of cards is shuffled and a card removed. This is found to be the deuce of diamonds. The index only is shown to the spectator. He calls the card aloud and at the same instance an assistant presents the magician with an envelope. Quick as a flash, the envelope changes to a card which happens to be the missing two of diamonds and on looking through the deck it is not found therein. The flap of the envelope permits of the rapid card change. The illustration shows why the deuce cannot be found. It was previously removed from the deck and the index of the tray of diamonds changed to a deuce. This card is forced.

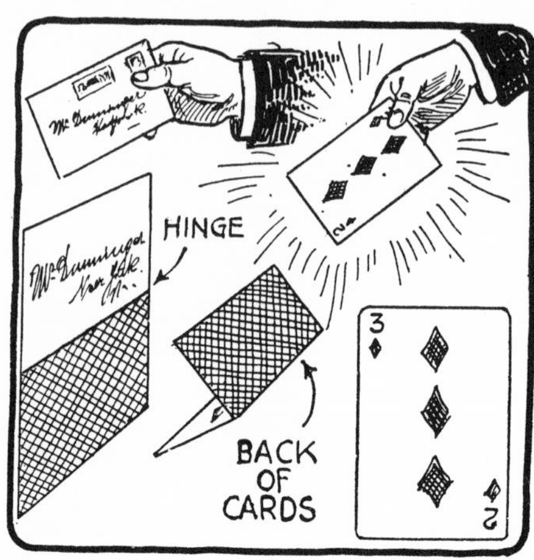

This diagram indicates how an envelope can be made so that it is converted almost instantaneously to a card.

Producing the Lighted Candle

Tricks with lighted candles are a usual favorite with the average audience and always have a tendency of convincing spectators of the magician's ability, because of the fact that he is considered clever who is capable of handling burning objects. After displaying both hands empty, he reaches into his vest pocket and withdraws one lighted candle after the other. The illustration describes the effect. The candles are mounted in a clip and as one after the other is withdrawn, it is lighted in the same fashion as an ordinary pocket lighter. If desired, the top can be a feke, which can be removed and the candles passed for examination after each one is produced.

Bill in Cigarette Trick

THIS is a very impressive after-dinner trick. The magician borrows a dollar bill and causes it to disappear (by means of a pull or any of the other methods previously mentioned). So as not to be different, he borrows a cigarette, then breaking this open, he withdraws the dollar bill previously vanished. The trick is performed by aid of the feke illustrated. A cigarette from which the tobacco has been removed is stuffed with a dollar bill, the numbers of which have been previously memorized. This cigarette is then put in the feke. When the performer borrows a cigarette, he substitutes it for one in the feke. In order to enhance the mystery, the performer on borrowing the dollar bill, reads its numbers aloud, but in reality calls off those numbers of his own concealed bill, which he has memorized.

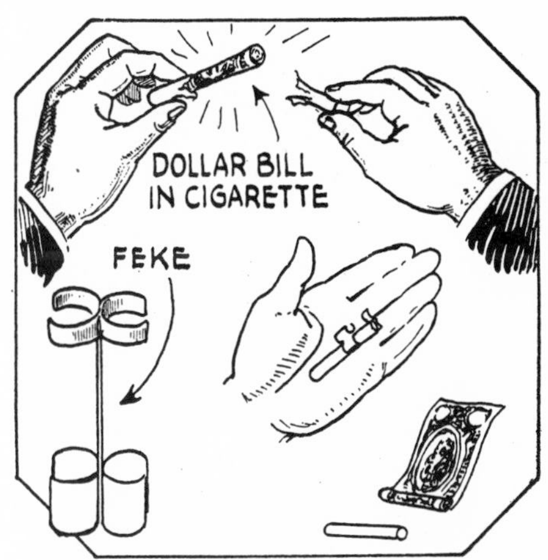

By means of the feke here illustrated, the performer can cause a dollar bill to appear in a borrowed cigarette.

The Enchanted Cylinder

IN this effect the performer makes a cylinder of paper about 3 inches in diameter and 8 or 9 inches tall. This is held in shape by a couple of clips. After the cylinder is examined, it is returned to the performer, who, holding it in his outstretched hand, reaches into the tube with his other hand, and mysteriously produces a large silk handkerchief. The cylinder is ordinary, but the feke constructed similar to the illustration, supports a cloth cup which holds the handkerchief. The bent arm of flesh-colored wire permits the feke to be moved well up into the cylinder. While this stunt appears to be very simple, in reality the effect which it produces on the audience is unusual, to say the least. The feke can be passed from hand to hand, if needed, and for that reason the stunt has puzzled experts.

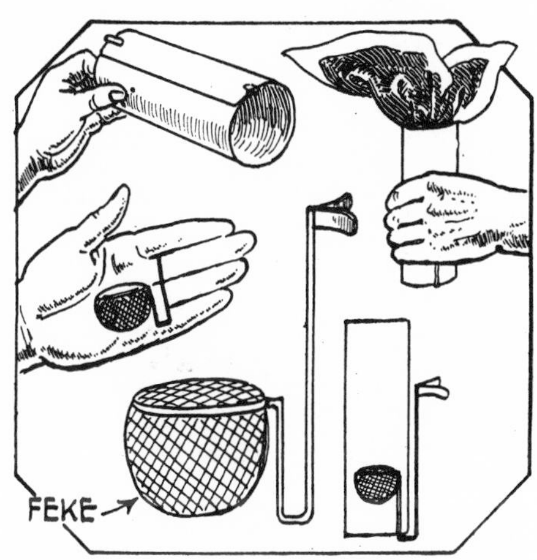

Even wizards are fooled by this handkerchief production easily accomplished by the feke shown.

The Magnetic Card

AN examined and an unprepared deck of cards is held fan-wise in the outstretched hand and offered to the spectator, who is requested to make a free selection, and remove the card thus chosen from the pack. Someone else is then asked to mark it with initials. The card is returned, shuffled into the deck, the magician rubs his finger across the top of the deck, and the chosen card mysteriously sticks to it. The effect is accomplished by aid of a small spring steel clip to which a needle point has been soldered. This clip is attached to the card as it is returned to the deck. It should fit the card firmly enough so that it will not shake loose in shuffling. The needle merely pricks the skin and consequently the card rises as the finger is lifted. The clip is removed from the card and palmed.

A clip attached to a card as indicated in this illustration causes the card to mysteriously cling to the finger.

Roses from Nowhere

Here is a system for producing a large bouquet of real roses from beneath a previously examined and totally unprepared foulard. As will be observed, the flowers are pinned to the back of a chair in such a way that when the silk thread is pulled by one or two assistants in the wings, the bouquet will rise up, so the magician can grasp it in an upright position. The distance of the magician from the chair depends entirely on his ability. Or if desired, the bouquet can be lifted in an inverted position, and carried forward under cover of the cloth to within a few feet of the footlights before the bouquet is produced in a most surprising manner.

Cut and Restored Card

AN ordinary brown manilla envelope, just large enough to hold a playing card, a card and a pair of scissors, are the only appurtenances necessary. The performer permits any member of

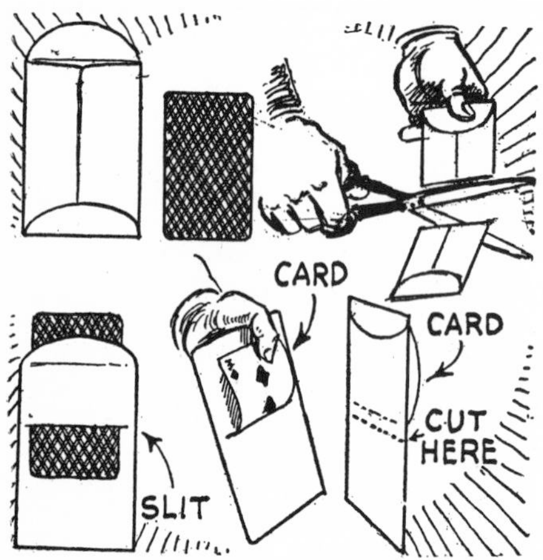

In this effect, a playing card is placed in an envelope cut in half and the playing card withdrawn whole. Illustration shows how it is done.

his audience to freely select a card. This is then initialed by the spectator and visibly placed into an envelope and sealed. Holding the envelope in one hand and the scissors in the other, the magician then divides the envelope in half. Picking up the two pieces, he holds them together, tears open the seal, and withdraws the playing card intact. The secret: The envelope is previously prepared with a slit cut crosswise into the back thereof. When inserting the card, it is made to project through this opening, and is bent over on itself preparatory to the cutting operation.

The Enchanted Cigar

AFTER having partaken of a few puffs of a cigar, the magician shows a new trick. Taking his silk handkerchief out of his pocket, he vanishes it by any method he might favor. Then removing the cigar, he carefully wraps it in a paper napkin, tears the napkin apart, and produces the handkerchief from the interior of the rolled napkin, the cigar having vanished. The secret: Two handkerchiefs are used. One of these is previously placed inside of the cigar which, as the illustration indicates, is made of aluminum in two halves suitably covered

A dummy cigar, suitably provided for receiving a handkerchief, mysteriously changes from one to the other as explained in the accompanying story.

with tobacco leaf to represent a real cigar. The front end is fitted with a cup for tobacco, and it is the tobacco in this end which is lighted and smoked. A tube leads from this cup receptacle, and conveys the smoke to the user's mouth.

Chameleon Ball

READERS looking for something new and different in ball effects will undoubtedly appreciate the trick here described. After performing a few tricks with ordinary red billiard balls, the

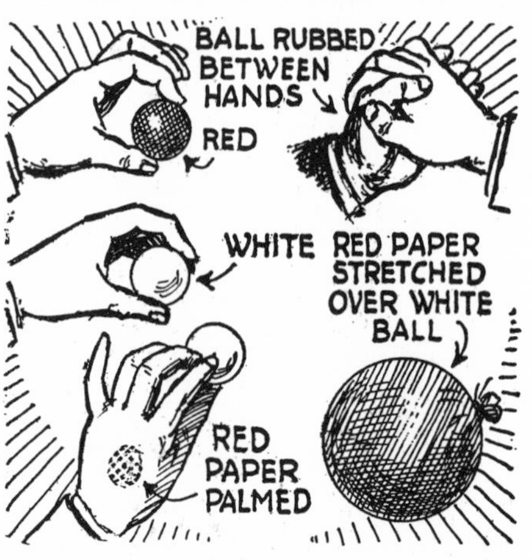

Here is a simple effect in which a red ball changes instantly to a white ball. The medium is thin tissue paper, stretched over the white ball as indicated.

magician bares his arms to his elbows, shows his hands on both sides to prove that they are free of preparation, and then taking a red billiard ball approximately two inches in diameter, he rubs this between his fingers, and mysteriously changes its color to a pearly white. The ball is immediately passed for examination.

Secret: An unprepared white ball is covered with a layer of red tissue, firmly drawn over it and then tied with a piece of string. When this is displayed at a short distance, it appears to be a red ball.

The Rising Cards

In this improved rising card effect a deck of cards is placed into the houlette containing a card chosen by the spectator. A rod is lightly touched against the back of the cards and sends them all flying up into the air. The houlette is turned 180°, presenting the back of the cards to the audience and the same action continues. Rotating the houlette again, the magician shows but one card left, which was the one chosen. By way of explanation the diagram above shows what goes on. The wand itself is of a mechanical construction and the spiral spring rotates a disc at the end which when made to lightly touch the cards, pushes them into the air. When it comes to the chosen card, it stops because the duplicate of the one forced is made of metal covered with a card on either side. Its weight makes it too heavy to be lifted by the wheel. Touching the rod to the front drives out all of the other cards.

Second Sight With Crayons

THIS is an absolutely new principle with which the magician presents a pleasing and mysterious experiment in second sight. A box of varied colored crayons and a borrowed derby hat are the only prerequisites. Someone in the audience is requested to select a color. The magician picks out the colored crayon from the box, writes a name on a piece of paper and then asks that that crayon, together with all the others be placed into the borrowed derby hat. He is now blindfolded and, picking out one crayon after the other, he finally calls out the color of the one selected crayon, as if mysteriously gifted with the power to know that this was the same crayon he had previously used. The secret is unusually simple. All crayons are covered with a paper wrapper. After one of the colors has been decided upon, the magician writes with it on a piece of paper and secretly breaks it beneath the paper wrapping. With a little practice, he can easily feel the break of the crayon as he holds it to his forehead. If repeated, the break must be made in a different place.

In this effect the break beneath the paper wrapper of a colored crayon indicates to the magician which one of the selected crayons he must correctly name. The trick can easily be arranged for.

New Obedient Apple

EVERYONE has seen the obedient ball in which a ball is made to slide down a string and mysteriously stop at command. This stunt as well as its operation is very well known, but for someone to pick up an apple and then thread a needle and string through that apple and repeat the same experiment is a much greater puzzle, and the stunt becomes fairly sensational. The operation of the trick is dependent entirely upon a small metal feke in the form of a curved tin tube illustrated in the diagram. This is secretly forced through the center of the fruit at an opportune moment or it may be threaded through the fruit at the time when the magician passes the needle and thread through it. The needle in this case is a flexible steel needle long enough to pass through the fruit and with it the string is threaded through the apple. Any time any of the spectators commands the fruit to stop in its downward fall, the apple does so. Tightening the string produces this effect. Many variations of this trick are, of course, possible to the magician.

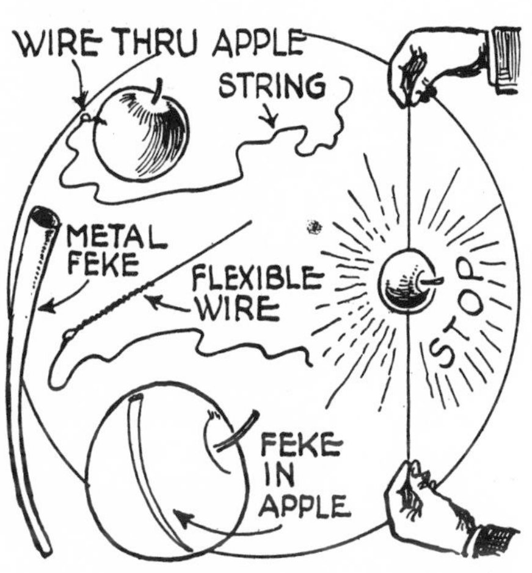

By aid of the metal feke placed into the apple and the string threaded through it, the performer can command the apple to stop midway in its fall. This is an excellent pocket trick.

THE ENCHANTED CANE

THIS experiment differs materially from the usual routine of magical mysteries. It requires no special paraphernalia. In effect the performer displays a large sheet of paper showing both sides thereof. He rolls this into a cone, then, holding this cone in front of him, he puts his hand down into the open mouth and extracts a full length cane which he taps to indicate its solidity and then passes out among the audience for free examination. In order to perform the effect, a straight cane with a knob at the upper end thereof is provided. This is previously concealed within a special pocket sewed within the performer's trouser leg. Thus suspended, the performer finds no difficulty in walking back and forth and need not arouse suspicion. During the act of rolling up the paper cone, he puts his hand inside and tears a slit through the paper through which the cane can be easily grasped and removed.

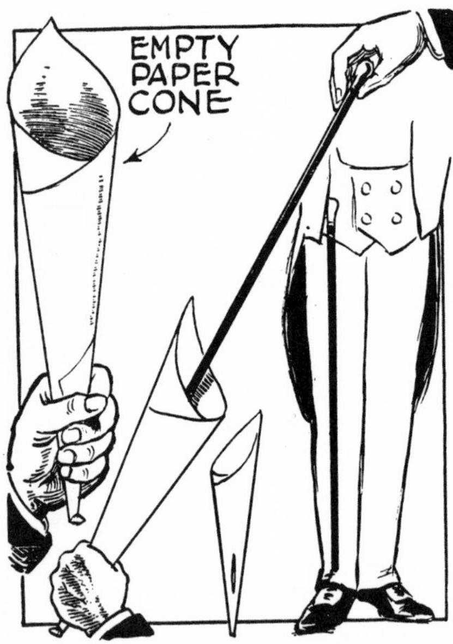

After rolling up a piece of paper into the form of a cone, the performer puts his hand into it and withdraws a regular walking cane. As will be observed, this has been previously concealed in the leg of his trousers.

THE DEMON REFLECTION

A SMALL hand mirror is passed for examination, and when found to be intact is returned to the wizard. A pack of playing cards is then fanned out and a spectator selects one and names its suit aloud. Let us assume that the trey of hearts has been chosen. A pocket handkerchief is next borrowed and the selected card is placed face upward on a small hand mirror. The mirror is then given to someone to hold. The affair is now covered with a handkerchief, and when the kerchief is removed the card is found to have mysteriously vanished. On looking through the deck, it is there again located. The explanation; two cards identical in suit are used. One of these is forced. It is left in the deck while apparently being removed, and the duplicate or prepared card is removed from the bottom of the pack. This duplicate is an ordinary card glued to a small mirror. When placed on the mirror frame it is turned by the magician under cover of the handkerchief.

A forced card is placed on the face of a mirror covered with a handkerchief and on removing the handkerchief, the card has disappeared!

CIGARETTES AND FINGER RING TRICK

THIS is an excellent pocket trick and can be presented as a spiritual effect. The magician borrows a finger ring, and in keeping with his policy of borrowing, he also borrows a cigarette. He pushes this cigarette through the finger ring, which is held lightly between the thumb and forefinger. Now, raising his hand and making mysterious passes, the cigarette remains suspended in the middle of the ring, and at command rises or falls! Having produced the effect several times, the magician returns both borrowed articles intact. The explanation is rather simple. An ordinary finger ring is used and the cigarette is attached to a thread with a pellet of wax. By moving the hand further away from the body, the cigarette is made to rise. When brought closer, the cigarette falls. This is due to the fact that the hair is attached to the vest button.

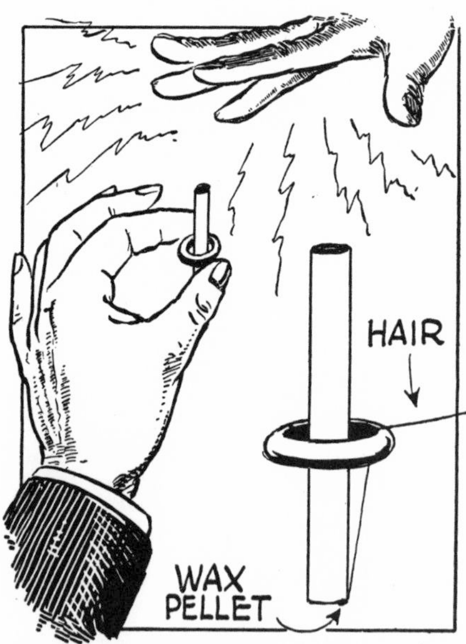

In this effect an ordinary cigarette is made to rise mysteriously in the air by what one can assume to be a mesmeric force. Actually a hair and a pellet of wax produce the effect.

A NEW CYLINDER TRICK

In this effect the magician makes an apple disappear and reappear as often as he desires. The only requisite is a cylinder larger than the object to be vanished and, of course, the magician's indispensable black thread. It will be observed that the thread passes through the side of the canister and is attached to the article to be vanished. By lifting the canister when the hand is held close to the body, the object will remain in sight. By stretching the arm out to full length, the object, of course, remains within the confines of the metal covering. Thus the effect can be repeated as often as desired.

CIGAR CASE TRICK

A case full of cigars is made to mystically change into a cigar case full of colored handkerchiefs. The construction of the case is responsible for the change.

Magicians favor tricks with silk handkerchiefs of various colors because they are pleasing to the eye, and they carry with them a popular appeal. The color blend also seems to satisfy the audience to a greater extent than some of the even more spectacular effects. The modern showman requires variety and variation, so here is a variation which can be employed and which does not take up much room. A leather cigar case of apparently the ordinary type is seen lying on the table. The magician shows it, draws a cigar therefrom, closes it, and vanishes several handkerchiefs, which are later found in the case.

Explanation: The construction of the case is responsible for the strange transformation. In reality, the box has two covers, and by simply turning the case around either compartment is brought into view. Half cigars are found on one side with one whole cigar extending down into the bottom, if so desired. This trick can also be produced with a small cigar case, making it an admirable pocket magical apparatus.

NEW LEMON TRICK

There are many ways of producing the effect wherein a coin is vanished and afterwards discovered inside a lemon. This has always been a favorite among the professional magicians, and even various contrivances have been adapted so that the amateur will have no difficulty in mastering the moves necessary to bring about the effective termination of the trick. The present system described, enables this stunt to be performed without any practice whatever, and will permit one or more coins to be produced from inside of a lemon. The knife with which the lemons are divided, has a double blade which is hollow and which provides space sufficient to hold several coins. These coins drop out through a cavity as indicated. Ordinary lemons are passed out for thorough examination and any one of them can be selected and marked, and then presented to the performer. On cutting the lemon he, of course, starts to cut with the end of the knife nearer the handle, and by properly tilting the knife as the tip moves down into the citrous fruit, the coins can be made to drop into the lemon.

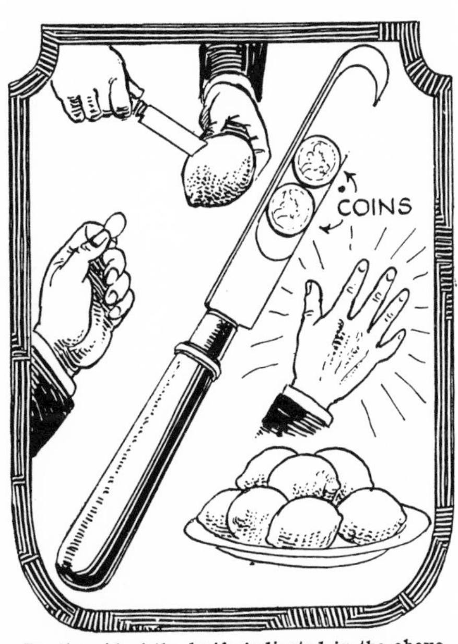

By the aid of the knife indicated in the above diagram, coins can be made to appear in a lemon, freely chosen by one of the spectators.

THE MYSTIC DECANTER

By the aid of a rubber hose and a bulb, the magician is able to control the movements of the glass stopper in the top of the decanter, and thus make it answer questions.

This effect is quite suitable for the stage or the drawing room. A seemingly ordinary decanter is exhibited, made entirely of glass. The mouth has the usual glass stopper, which is inserted by the wizard, who claims that the decanter is occasionally invaded by a spirit and this spirit causes the glass stopper to jump about, producing a series of clicks. Having made friends with the spirit, the magician has been able to get him to answer various questions, by the usual sign—one click meaning no, and two, yes. Questions are then asked of the audience and the answer is obtained from the jumping stopper.

Explanation: The diagram explains the system. A concealed assistant controls the action of this stopper through a long rubber tube, terminating in a rubber bulb. By pressing on the bulb, he is able to force air into the decanter, which causes the loose-fitting stopper to bounce up and down, in direct response to the puffs of air. The decanter being heavier and having a hole in the bottom, is not shifted by the air pressure. It can also be operated by the foot.

A CRYSTAL CASKET MYSTERY

An empty glass box is exhibited to the audience. Four tumblers are then placed on a table and the box is then placed on top of these tumblers. The magician explains that inasmuch as the casket and the tumblers are quite transparent, it is impossible for anything to enter the box, elevated above the table-top. Nevertheless, he produces in large numbers, flags, hundreds of ribbons, paper, handkerchiefs of different colors, etc. The effect is phenomenal, but easily explained. One of the glasses supporting the box is bottomless and is what is technically known as a mirror glass. That is, a mirror is cut to fit the glass and placed within it. The glass thus appears entirely empty at all times, yet plenty of action can occur behind the mirror portion. All of the flags, ribbons, etc., being lightly fastened together, it becomes a simple matter to fill the box with the decorations from the false table-top in which they repose. The apparatus and the effect is illustrated in the diagrams above.

CARD PRODUCTION

The hand is first shown empty. Suddenly it is full of cards. The effect is accomplished by having a deck of cards in the sleeve connect with the finger ring via a thread. The thread pulls the cards out.

THIS trick has never previously been published, and will be found a welcome number to those desirous of something really different. The conjurer holds his right hand far away from his body. Slowly and distinctly, he shows both back and front of his hand, fingers wide apart. Reaching into space, a handful of playing cards mysteriously make their appearance in the wizard's outstretched hand.

The diagram clearly illustrates the modus operandi. A number of cards are held together with a small clip. These cards are then secreted in a pocket, which has been formed in the lining upon the inside of the performer's sleeve. A piece of fine silk thread is tied to the clip, and passes through a small eyelet of the magician's finger ring. This ring is worn upon the middle finger. The free end of the thread is tied to the magician's waistcoat button. Moving the hand forward draws the cards out of the sleeve and brings them safely to the magician's palm.

WATCH IT

HERE is an excellent impromptu trick. The effect is that a watch is taken out of the vest pocket and suspended from the chain. In this position the performer removes it from the clasp which holds it to the chain, then invisibly throws it into the air and apparently catches it on the chain again, down which it is seen to slide, coming to a stop at the bottom. In practice, the stunt is accompished in the following manner. There are two watches attached to the chain. When the performer removes one watch, he at the same time conceals in the palm of his left hand the other watch, of identical construction. The ring on this second watch is soldered at an angle directly to the stem so as not to interfere with any downward motion of the watch as it is dropped. Thus, after removing the watch from the bottom of the chain, it is apparenty tossed toward the chain again, but in reality it is palmed, with the aid of a loop of flesh colored thread.

A watch chain is removed from the bottom of a chain, tossed in the air and is caught by the chain, down which it slides to the bottom. Actually two watches are employed.

HANDKERCHIEF TRICK

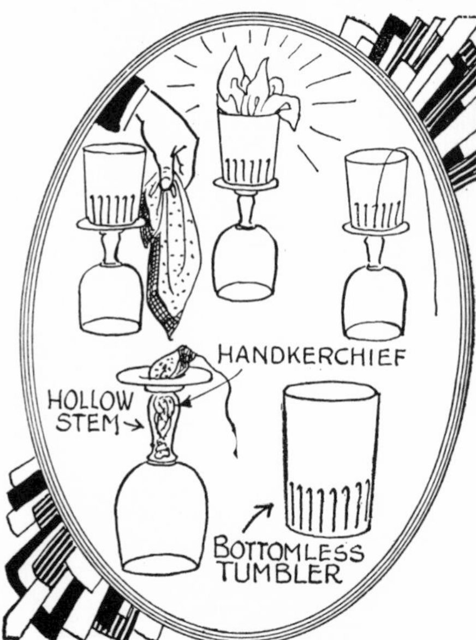

In this effect, a stem glass is turned upside-down and a tumbler placed on top of it. A moment later, a handkerchief previously vanished appears in the tumbler. The stunt is accomplished by the aid of a hollow stem glass, and a bottomless tumbler.

THE effect to the audience is approximately as follows. A transparent glass goblet is placed mouthdown on the table. A tumbler is stood on the foot. A silk handkerchief is now made to vanish and mystically appears as quick as a flash, in the tumbler which a moment ago was empty.

In presenting this trick, both tumblers are prepared. The silk handkerchief is a duplicate of the one that is vanished. It is pushed into the hollow stem of a goblet. In order to prevent this handkerchief from being seen, the stem is first lined with tinfoil. At a short distance it appears that the stem is transparent. The other piece of apparatus necessary in this effect is a bottomless tumbler. This is of the regulation type used in many different mysteries. The handkerchief is drawn into this bottomless tumbler from the stem of the glass by an assistant, who, at the proper moment, pulls it into view. Of course, a thin black thread is used.

THE PENETRATING HANDKERCHIEF

In this effect a candle is seen in a candlestick. The magician pushes a handkerchief over the flame, extinguishing it, and then, with a little additional pressure, he forces the candle clear through the kerchief. He again lights the tip of the candle. A short time later he removes the kerchief again, and relights the candle, returning the handkerchief intact. The effect is accomplished by having a candle fitted into a holder and so arranged that it can slide down in the candlestick for a limited distance. A weighted piece of candle with a needle is poked through the handkerchief unobserved by the audience and this is then put on top of the candle in the candlestick. The weight of this small section pushes the candle down, preventing the effect of a change in height. Of course, the feke is palmed both times, but this is easy under cover of the kerchief.

THE BEWITCHED CIGARETTE

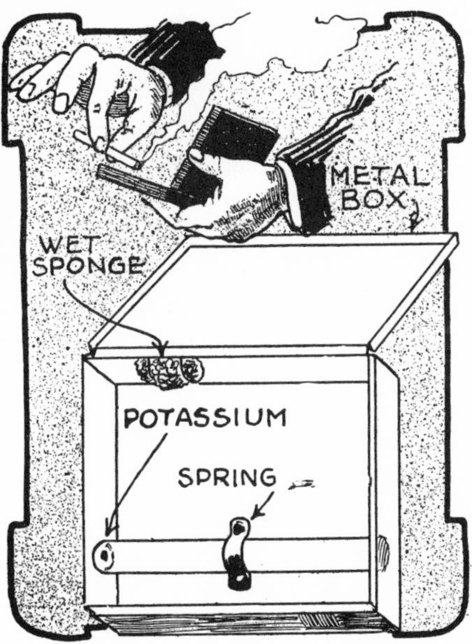

The cigarette can be made to light itself and can actually be removed from the cigarette box lit, if the method here illustrated is employed. A wet sponge and a piece of potassium serve to light it.

In concluding any sort of a cigarette vanishing or producing act, which can be composed of those many different styles of vanishes and productions, previously explained in this publication, a lit cigarette can be vanished, and two or three minutes later it can again be produced, still lit, from the interior of a cigarette case. This cigarette case will also be useful as a small pocket trick for the after-dinner trickster. The method in which the effect is carried out is very simple. One or more cigarettes are clipped to the interior of a metal box by a spring clip. In the tips of each of these cigarettes there is a small piece of metallic potassium. As the magician opens the lid of the box, it is not at all difficult to twist the cigarette to make it contact with the wet sponge placed within the box, which in turn causes the potassium to ignite and lights the cigarette. Care should be exercised in handling the potassium.

NEW KERCHIEF CYLINDER

This is a clever deception rather simple to execute and quite effective. The conjurer first exhibits a plain glass cylinder, which appears to be quite clear and unquestionably empty. With a sharp movement into space, a large silk handkerchief is mystically caught in thin air and it finds its way into the cylinder, completely filling it. Both silk and tube are immediately passed for examination. By way of explanation, the silk was rolled into a small compact and concealed beneath the lapel of the performer's coat. A fine silk thread was attached to a corner of this handkerchief, passed through the tube, and then tied to a coat or vest button. With a quick movement of the cylinder in an upward direction, the silk is brought from behind the coat lapel, flashes in the air and then finds its way into the cylinder. The thread is now quickly broken, and the entire is passed to the audience for examination.

A glass cylinder quite clear and empty will be found to suddenly contain a handkerchief apparently caught out of thin air. A piece of thread passing through the cylinder and the kerchief beneath the coat lapel permit of this effect.

HYPNOTIZED STRAW

Next time you go to a soda fountain you can demonstrate to your friends your ability to hypnotize a soda straw and cause it to rise up in the palm of your hand provided that you have previously attached the gimmick illustrated.

Apparently the only apparatus used in this trick is a soda straw such as is ordinarily found at soda fountains. This is placed flat upon the palm of the magician's hand, and after a few hypnotic passes are made over it with the other hand, the straw is seen to mysteriously and slowly float or move upward, until it stands in an upright position. It can be left in this position or again permitted to gradually sink to the palm. At any moment it may be passed for examination. The secret is exceedingly simple. A small plug made of light wood is just large enough to hold the end of the straw. The point of a needle is driven into this plug. Before demonstrating the trick, the needle point is made to pass into the skin of the palm of the hand. By stretching the palm, the plug rises; relaxing causes it to fall. A soda straw being much lighter, this stunt is a vast improvement over the old pencil trick, in which the weight of the pencil made the operation of the trick practically impossible.

The Elusive Bottle

Snappy effects are quite the vogue with the up-to-date conjurer. In this particular stunt, an assistant brings forth a bottle of Volstead's departed spirits. The conjurer places a kerchief over the top of the bottle; then, apparently lifting the bottle, he causes it to vanish in air. The stunt is performed in the following fashion. The bottle itself is merely a sheet of celluloid painted to imitate a bottle and curled to further increase this illusion. Its shape is maintained by a hook at the back edges. The bottle is hinged to a tray. The handkerchief is prepared with a disk the same size as the mouth of the bottle. When placing the handkerchief over the bottle, the hook is released, the bottle falling flat to the tray, then the bottle is apparently lifted by holding the disk in the handkerchief. Grasping the corner and snapping it completes the vanish.

The Plate Eater

THE magician patters about East Indian tribes who feast upon stones, metal and the like. He picks up a large white china plate, and without hesitation, apparently, bites off a large piece. The action produces a loud snap as though plate breaks. The magician then seems to swallow the piece chewed out and holding the plate in front of his stomach, he rubs the missing section with his fingers whereupon the plate is once again mysteriously restored to it original form. Secret: An irregular flat piece of metal is slid over the edge of the plate just before the magician puts the plate into his mouth. This makes it seem that a piece has been chewed out of the plate when the latter is held in front of the coat. The snap is produced by clicking a coin against the back of the plate, and restoration, by palming the metal piece.

Magnetic Control

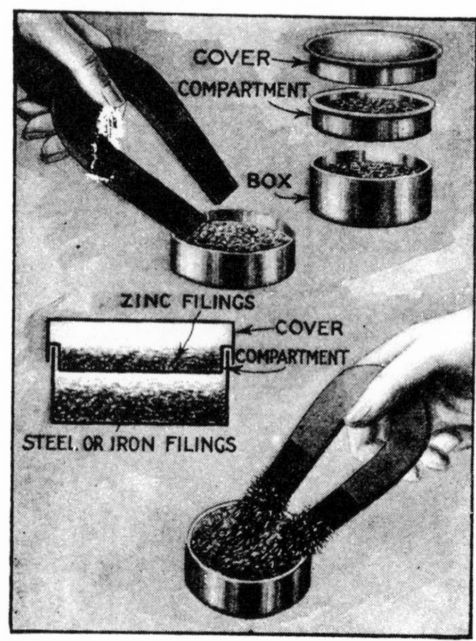

A HORSESHOE magnet is passed for inspection. The wizard then hands members in his audience a small pill-box filled with metal filings. Strangely the metal filings are not attracted to the magnet. The magician then passes his hands over the steel, and plunging it into the box he causes the metal filings to adhere to it. Secret: The magnet is of the ordinary variety, the pill-box is double. The top compartment contains zinc filings; the bottom compartment used by the magician contains steel or iron filings. The spectators test the first compartment. The magician uses the second.

Phantom Cigarettes

THE magician, feeling desirous of smoking a cigarette, reaches for his case and finds it empty. Pushing the drawer of a match-box open, he discovers that this too is empty. Someone is sure to remark that he, being a magician, might produce one from empty space, or the magician can assume that he heard such a remark, forcing the words upon the lips of one of the audience. Reaching into the air, he produces a burning cigarette. Secret: The cigarette case and match-box are purposely left empty so as to give the performer an opportunity of doing the trick. Actually, a lighted cigarette is supported behind the match-box, on a bent needle or pin protruding therefrom. When the magician picks up the match-box he gains possession of the cigarette. The cigarette can be concealed until the very instant of its production from the trick match-box.

Mystic Ball

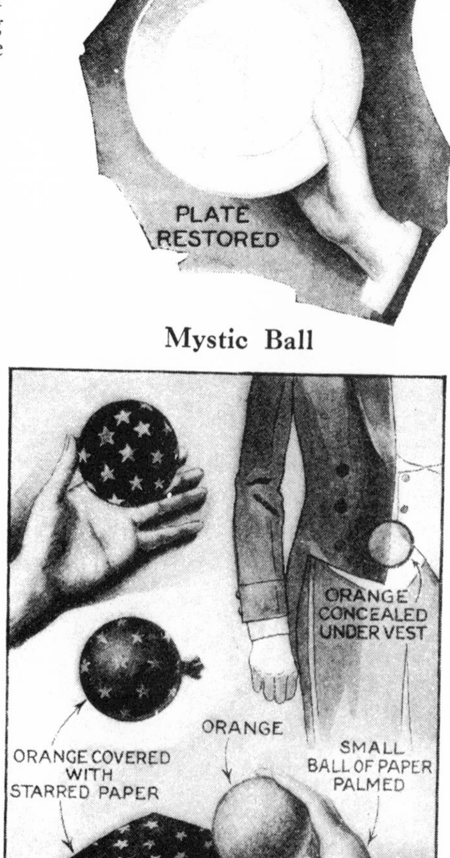

THE magician passes a sphere for inspection. This proves to be a black ball decorated with gold stars. Returning to the platform, he bares his arms to the elbows, rolls the ball between his palms, and when again displayed it is found to be an orange. Secret: The ball itself is the size of an orange and has been decorated to conform with the pattern on black paper, which is used to cover an orange concealed beneath the vest. The ball is substituted for the orange and the paper is removed under cover of the palm.

The Spirit Voice

THE would-be medium tells her spectators that she is about to demonstrate spirit messages and independent voices even after having her mouth stuffed with cotton, and covered with a tightly drawn handkerchief. The lights are turned out and voices are heard. A phonograph is built into the top of the table and the starting mechanism is cleverly concealed. The record is especially made and has different voices recorded thereon.

Solid Through Solid

THE magician exhibits a glass tumbler and to prove that it is unprepared he fills it with water. He then pours the water back into the pitcher and borrowing a lady's handkerchief. he tucks it into the glass. Making a paper cylinder, he covers the glass therewith, and then picks up both glass and paper cover. He now proceeds to demonstrate that the tumbler does not interfere in the least with the handkerchief which is pulled right through the bottom. The secret lies in the fact that an oval hole has been cut in the side of the glass through which the handkerchief can be pulled. This hole is covered with the thumb when the glass contains water.

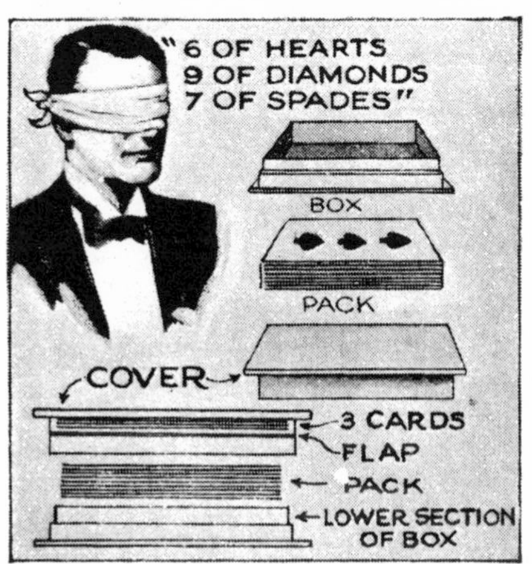

Come and Go Billiard Ball

EVERY amateur delights in demonstrating tricks which would impress the audience as being the result of years of practice. This billiard ball trick gives the desired impression. The ball is really a half ball and has a disk slightly larger than the diameter of the ball, glued to its back surface. The disk is covered with velvet. If this ball is held between the fingers, and then turned so that the velvet side faces the audience, and the hand is held in front of some dark clothing, the ball will seem to have disappeared.

X-Ray Card Trick

AN ordinary pack of playing cards is passed for examination, shuffled thoroughly, and the spectator then places the deck in a card case. The card case is covered, the magician blindfolded, and then upon command, the box is opened. The spectator then removes the cards one by one as the magician correctly names them. The secret lies in the fact that three or more cards, previously memorized, are secreted in the cover of the box and hidden from view by a small flap. When closing the box, the flap drops and the prearranged cards fall in place on top of the deck.

Mental Marvel

Large audiences throughout this country have been mystified by this trick, originated by the writer. At present, various so-called "dealers in magic" are charging fabulous prices for the secret. Effect: The mind reader exhibits two clean slates. One of them is handed to a spectator with the instruction to go to the far side of the hall and draw any picture he desires with the chalk with which he is provided. While doing this, the "mental marvel" sketches a picture upon the duplicate slate. When the spectator returns, both slates are held up for examination, and to the amazement of the spectators, the drawings upon them are found to be identical. Secret: The slate handed to the volunteer is apparently clean, yet upon close examination one will find a message lightly written with slate pencil. It reads, "Kindly draw this picture and we both will get a good laugh." Thus, if you are clever enough to pick the right assistant, he will do as the message indicated. Both he and the magician will find much amusement in the thunderous applause, and the assistant will not acknowledge his complicity to any except closest friends.

Materializations

THIS is an interesting spirit effect. The wizard is stripped of his clothing and examined to prove that no apparatus is concealed about his person. After dressing in a borrowed suit if desired, he is securely bound in a seated position to an ordinary office chair. The lights are extinguished and a few moments thereafter a small sphere of a ghostly green color becomes visible, gradually grows larger and takes on the form of a face. After a few minutes, the sphere again shrinks and disappears. The secret lies in the fact that a small toy balloon painted with a non-poisonous luminous paint was concealed in the mouth of the performer; the balloon, on being blown up, produces the materialization. The face should be artistically finished.

Even though the magician has been thoroughly searched and securely bound, he can materialize a ghost in a dark-room séance.

Demon Swordsmanship

With the aid of a card, on the back of which a piece of cloth has been pasted, the magician can catch a card in air on the point of a previously examined sword.

ALL kinds of mechanical swords have been constructed for catching a previously selected card in midair, but this is the first trick in which the sword can be passed for examination before and after presentation. The effect is briefly as follows: A card is selected from a pack, shuffled into the pack again and the spectator, upon request, tosses the entire deck into the air. The wizard thrusts the point of the sword among the falling cards and mysteriously catches the chosen card. Secret: The card is forced. A duplicate has been prepared by pasting a piece of cloth of the same color and design as the carpet upon the back. When the card is faced down on the carpet, it is quite invisible. The magician pushes the sword point into the card on the floor and then brings this up among those in the air.

The Talkative Coin

IN previous articles in this series, I have mentioned "talking" coins wherein the coin beneath the cover is the one manipulated. The effect: A coin is examined, marked and dropped into a glass which is placed by the spectator on an end table. A handkerchief is then borrowed and used to cover the glass. Any questions now asked are answered by clinks of the coin. At any moment the coin can be examined. The secret:

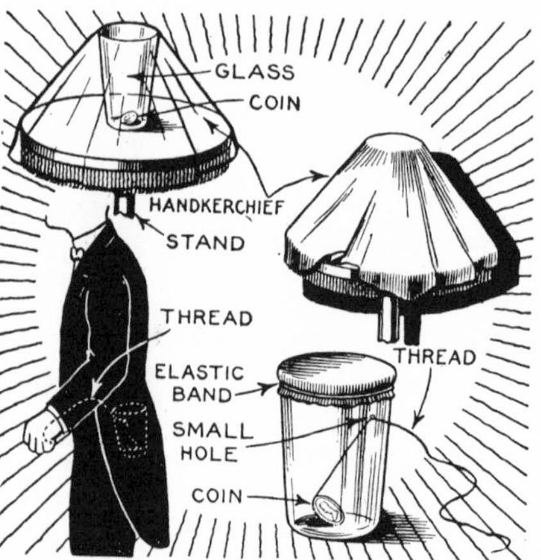

A duplicate coin in a glass, concealed in the performer's hip pocket, produces the sound which spectators believe comes from a glass and coin on the table.

All of the paraphernalia on the table is absolutely innocent of deception. The performer has prepared himself by placing a duplicate tumbler in his hip pocket. This contains a coin attached to a thin thread which runs down his sleeve and is fastened at the vest. By moving the string the duplicate coin in the pocket is made to produce the sound.

The small electric candlelight in the center of the table answers questions by flashing once for "No" and twice for "Yes." The light is under control of the magician, through the agency of the "plate lifter."

The Answering Light

The Disappearing Water

Enchanted Tape

● AN electric lamp, consisting of a tubular fixture, containing a battery, with a switch operable from the bottom, and a small globe, socketed beneath an inverted glass hood (such as illustrated) has recently been placed upon the market, and is securable at every large electrical supply house.

HOOK HOOK
WATER
12"
WATER CONTAINER HUNG ON ASSISTANT'S BACK
LOOSE FITTING BOTTOM
5"

Water is made to vanish from a canister by the simple apparatus illustrated in the above diagram.

Should the mechanically inclined reader, however, prefer, the diagram will enable him to construct one of these, with but little difficulty. As will be noticed, the lighting and extinguishing of the bulb depends upon the plunger-like projecting peg arrangement at the bottom of the fixture. An excellent "spirit" effect is obtained by causing this light to mystically go on and off, guided, apparently, only by the will of the wonder worker. The lamp is set in the center of a large drawing room table, with the hands of a selected committee resting upon the edge of the table, as illustrated. This arrangement is similar to the one common in so-called spiritualistic circles, when the palms of spectators are placed upon the table, to cause "spirit raps." In this case, however, no spirits are necessary (unless they be of the bottled variety). The magician has secreted beneath the table cover, what is known as a plate-lifting device; this can also be secured in practically any novelty shop. It consists of a long rubber tube, with a small rubber bag attached to one end of the tube, and a small rubber ball, to the other. The magician, who sits at one end of the table, secretly controls the light by pressure upon the rubber ball, concealed beneath the palm of his hand. The rubber bag attached to the tube, naturally rests directly beneath the plunger switch of the lamp; and when it is expanded by pressure on the ball, it closes the switch which lights the lamp.

For the next effect, a Chinese canister is shown, apparently unprepared. It consists of a metal tube, twelve inches high, and about five inches in diameter. An assistant enters, carrying a large transparent pitcher containing water, which the wizard proceeds to empty into the container. The empty pitcher is handed to the attendant, who then exits. The wizard draws attention to the difficulty of the problem he is about to present. Without any false moves whatsoever, he runs his arm with considerable force, into, and completely through the canister, forcing the bottom off; this drops to the floor. All that

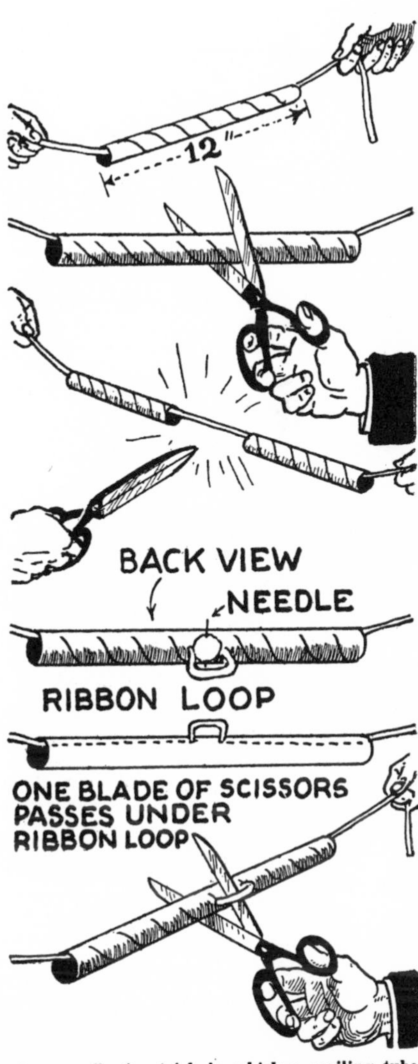

A very effective trick in which a mailing tube is cut in half, while the ribbon which passes through it, from end to end, remains intact.

now remains is an empty tube, which is passed for inspection at once. The liquid contents have completely vanished.

Explanation: An inner metal lining is secretly contained inside the canister. It is this inner section which really receives and retains the water. Several hooks are soldered to the upper edge of this inner lining, and project about half an inch over the outer edge of the cylinder. When presenting the illusion, and after emptying the water into the canister, the pitcher is returned to the assistant. During this action, the cylinder is for a moment hidden from the audience's view, behind the attendant's back. It is during this brief interval that the magician finds the opportunity of hooking the inner cylinder to the attendant's coat. With a small amount of practice, this move can be accomplished with perfection, and so quickly that the act cannot possibly be discovered. The attendant, in leaving the stage, naturally walks off, being careful that the load upon his back is not discovered. This leaves the empty cylinder, with a removable bottom, in the magician's hands. With a bit of showmanship, he then concludes the experiment.

In the Enchanted Tape trick, a length of tape (about a yard and a half long, and an inch wide), a pair of scissors, a needle and a 12-inch mailing tube are all the paraphernalia necessary to perform one of the most startling and mystifying of magical tricks. The tape running through the tube is exhibited, and two spectators are requested to stand at opposite ends, each holding one of the ends of the tape. Using a pair of scissors, the magician deliberately cuts the mailing tube and its contents in half. Strange as it may seem, the tube, divided in half, remains upon the tape, which is still intact. The pieces of tubing are removed, and the tape passed for immediate inspection.

Explanation: Before presenting the trick, a small piece had secretly been cut out of the back of the tube. The tape is threaded, as in the diagram, to enable a loop of the tape to be pulled through the hole, and project upon the outside of the tube. The piece cut out is put back in place and held there by a needle, which is quite invisible at a short distance. In the act of cutting the tube in half, one blade of the scissors is secretly passed under the loop, enabling the magician to cut the tube, without injury to the tape. The needle naturally drops to the floor, unnoticed.

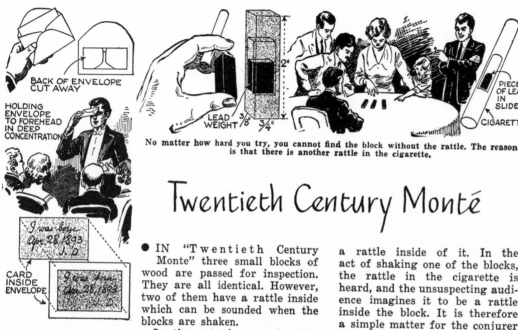

A simple method of reading slips in envelopes.

No matter how hard you try, you cannot find the block without the rattle. The reason is that there is another rattle in the cigarette.

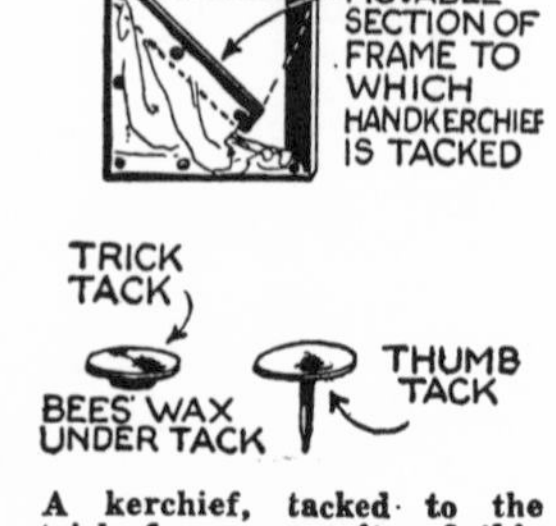

A kerchief, tacked to the trick frame, permits of this illusion.

Twentieth Century Monté

● IN "Twentieth Century Monte" three small blocks of wood are passed for inspection. They are all identical. However, two of them have a rattle inside which can be sounded when the blocks are shaken.

In the act of presenting the trick, the wizard shakes the block, and then mixes the three about, asking the spectators to find the block without the rattle. Try as they will, this is more or less impossible; as they always seem to pick the wrong one.

When presenting the trick, the magician nonchalantly holds a cigarette between his fingers. The cigarette is mechanical, being constructed from a piece of tubing, with a rattle inside of it. In the act of shaking one of the blocks, the rattle in the cigarette is heard, and the unsuspecting audience imagines it to be a rattle inside the block. It is therefore a simple matter for the conjurer to deceive the spectators. All the blocks have a rattle when he picks them up. Needless to state, he must personally know the exact position of the plain block.

Simple "Thought-Reading" Method

● IN this thought-reading effect, several small cards are passed to the spectators; and questions or statements are written on them during the magician's absence from the room. Upon his return, he places the cards in small envelopes, holding the written sides downward, so that it is quite impossible for him to read the cards. Holding the envelopes for a moment to his head, he enters an apparent trance, and mysteriously becomes familiar with the various questions and statements that have been secretly written.

The *modus operandi* of this excellent thought-reading trick is exceptionally simple. Sections are cut away from the back of the envelopes (as illustrated) unknown to the spectators. Thus the wizard can easily read what has been written upon the cards, during the act of holding the envelope to his head.

The affair is then placed in a paper bag; and the magician at once proceeds to push several solid objects, such as a cane, stick, and pencil through the bag and apparently through the kerchief. Yet, upon removing the frame from the paper bag, the kerchief is found still affixed to the frame, and not damaged at all.

The upper section of the frame has a movable slab, as illustrated. Thus the handkerchief can be secretly pushed out of place, permitting the solid objects to pass through the paper bag, unobstructed. One of the thumbtacks really has no point, but instead, only a piece of wax, which causes it to cling to the kerchief.

Elusive Cannon Ball

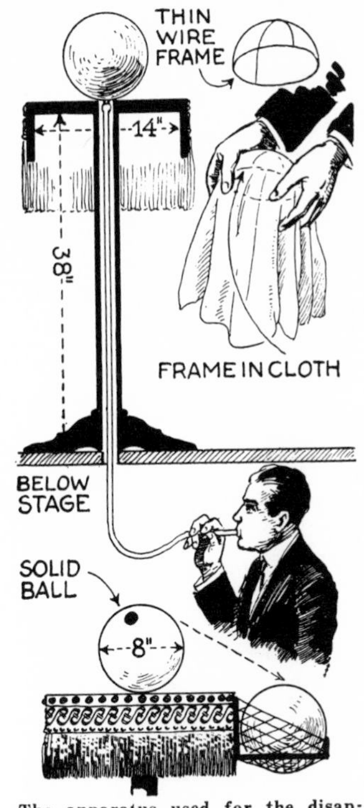

The apparatus used for the disappearing ball.

● IN the "Elusive Cannon Ball" effect, a wooden sphere, eight inches in diameter, is examined. The magician carries it back to the stage and, in order to further prove that no substitution has been made, strikes it several times upon a table top, proving conclusively that the solid ball is actually being used. He now covers it with a large silk cloth, and carries it across the stage to a small undraped side stand. Placing it upon the top of the stand, the cloth is again removed, proving that the ball is still there. It is once more covered and, at the magician's command, the cover is seen to slowly sink, the ball apparently diminishing. The cloth is removed and the large sphere is found to have mysteriously and completely vanished.

The solid ball, after being struck upon the table top, in the act of proving it solid, is covered with the cloth. Beneath this cover the ball is secretly permitted to roll into a *savante* (or bag) attached to the back of the table. A thin wire frame, sewed into the cloth (which is really two squares of cloth, sewed together around the edges, with the frame concealed between them), is carried across the stage, and placed upon the side stand. An assistant, concealed below the stage, blows up a toy balloon, affixed to the free end of a rubber hose, as illustrated. It is really this balloon which the audience sees, and imagines to be the solid wooden sphere, when the cloth is lifted. The ball is again covered, and the understage assistant allows the air to escape through the rubber hose, permitting the balloon to diminish, and (apparently) finally vanish.

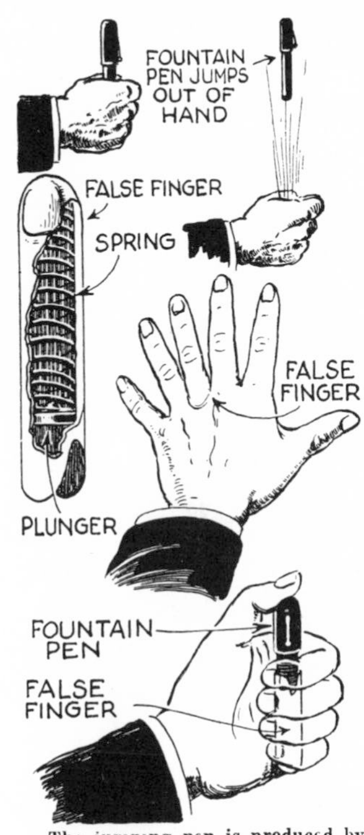

The jumping pen is produced by the spring in the false finger.

How a playing card is made to apparently appear in the envelope mounted on the stand.

The Jumping Fountain Pen

The wizard, after showing both hands quite empty and unprepared, closes the fingers of his right hand to form a fist. With his left hand, he proceeds to slowly push a fountain pen or pencil, half-way down into the fist, the upper part protruding. At his command, the fountain pen mysteriously leaps high into the air, and he catches it upon its descent. It is at once passed for inspection. Any pen or pencil may be used, and the experiment may be successfully repeated as often as desired.

The magician wears a false finger (what is professionally known as an "extra finger") made out of a piece of brass tubing, and painted flesh-color, to resemble his own. Worn between the second and third fingers of his left hand, it is quite unnoticed at a short distance, when the fingers of both hands spread wide apart, are nonchalantly displayed.

A very weak spring, with a plunger top, is concealed inside the finger. Thus, in presenting the trick, the finger is held in position secretly in the closed hand, so that the pen, being pushed into it forces the plunger down. The pressure of the thumb and first finger, upon the pen, prevent it from flying into space, until the leap is desired. At the conclusion of the trick, the finger is secretly pocketed or palmed, as the performer chooses.

Rapid-Transit Playing Card

A small stand (of the design illustrated) is located on the magician's table. An envelope is freely chosen, from a stack of twelve, which have been passed for inspection. The chosen envelope is then sealed and, without exchange, is placed in position upon the stand. The magician places a strong electric lamp reflector directly in back of the apparatus, so that the rays of the lamp, penetrating through the envelope, offer conclusive proof that there is nothing whatsoever concealed inside it. A playing card is chosen from a deck and, after the suit is called aloud, the card is torn into several small pieces; which are stuffed into the funnel-shaped tube attachment of a conjurer's pistol. The wizard points the gun at the stand and envelope, and fires. Instantly, the playing card, mysteriously restored, is seen inside the envelope; the rays of the strong light clearly silhouette the mysterious presence of the card. The envelope is removed from the stand; an end is torn therefrom, and the playing card is passed for inspection.

The stand is mechanical. A card, the duplicate of the one originally "forced" on the chooser, is concealed in the base. Two small rods, working upon springs, and hidden behind the two posts of the stand, carry the card into view, behind the envelope, at the desired moment. A pin, tied to a thin silk thread, the free end of which is in the hands of an off-stage assistant, enables the magician to regulate the appearance of the card. When the end of the envelope is torn open, the card is really drawn from behind the envelope, rather than from inside of it; this deception, however, is impossible to detect.

Cigarette Miracle • Indian Cocoanut Trick

"Palm smoking" a cigarette.

● THE "Cigarette Miracle" is an extremely interesting impromptu experiment, easily performed, and one which is sure to cause considerable astonishment. The wizard explains that he has been smoking too many cigarettes, and his physician has advised him to cut down upon the quantity. Like the average cigarette smoker, however, he finds it difficult to keep away from them; and so, instead of putting the cigarette in his mouth, he smokes them by simply holding one in his hands. He therefore borrows a cigarette —not that it makes any difference so far as the trick is concerned but, since the greater part of the cigarette will be wasted, it may just as well belong to someone else. Having lighted the cigarette, it is held in your hands in the manner shown in the diagram. Keep the palms pressed firmly together and, by slightly opening and shutting them, they are converted into a sort of bellows, with the cigarette for a nozzle. With little practice, you will find that you can smoke a cigarette quite easily in this manner; although naturally the onlookers get all the enjoyment out of it. A pipe may be smoked in this manner, with a little additional practise.

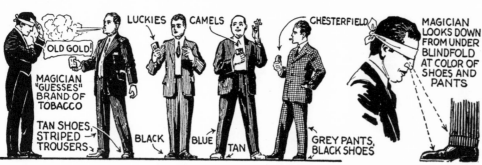

In the next experiment, four members of the audience —all absolute strangers to the wizard—are directed to come upon the stage, having been chosen because they are individual possessors of different brands of cigarettes—for example, we will say, the four representative brands—Camels, Luckies, Chesterfields and Old Golds. The magician is now securely blindfolded with a borrowed handkerchief

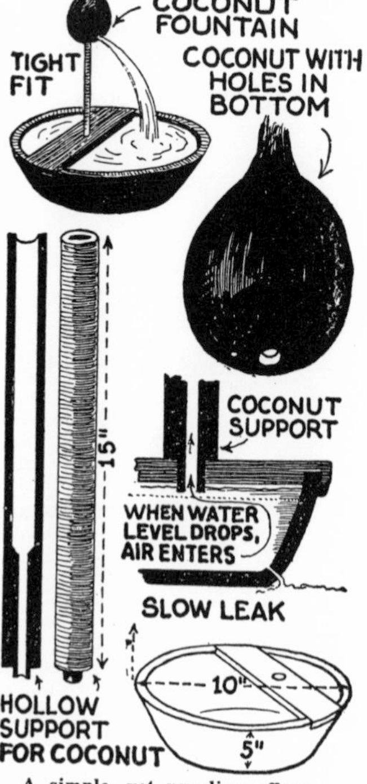

A simple, yet puzzling effect.

Magician professes to be able to tell the name of the cigarette by its smoke. The secret lies in associating the shoes with the type of smokes.

and the committee is requested to light their cigarettes, and, in any rotation, or order, they choose, blow the smoke toward the blindfolded wizard. Strangely enough, the magician calls the name of the cigarette of each smoker, claiming to be able to define the difference through the smoke.

The explanation is extremely simple. The magician secretly observes the shoes and trousers of each of the committee members, and associates them with the cigarettes they are holding. This is done before he is blindfolded. He further sees that the blindfold is placed high above his nose, so that he can look down along the bridge of his nose and see the floor. As any of the committee comes close to the magician, the wizard has to observe his shoes and trousers and thereby identify the brand of cigarette held by the individual and not of course, distinguish it by the smoke as the audience is led to believe.

The Indian cocoanut trick is a mystery said to be well known among Indian "fakirs" but, strangely, very few American and European conjurors are familiar with its secret. The apparatus consists of a cocoanut shell, a stick, and a small bowl made of hard wood. The cocoanut has two holes positioned as illustrated. The diagram also shows the construction of the stick, together with the details of the construction of the bowl. The Hindoo places the boat in an upright position upon the sand and then inserts the stick into the small hole in the seat running across the bowl. Both the bowl and cocoanut are filled with water and, by placing his thumb momentarily over the hole, the wizard inverts the cocoanut and forces the upright stick into the larger hole. Standing at some distance from the apparatus, he utters a mysterious command and the water mystically spouts out of the cocoanut onto the bowl, stopping at the wizard's wish. The experiment is repeated several times at intervals and the water spout always appears mysteriously and again stops at command.

The secret consists of a small hole drilled in the bottom of the bowl. Through this water is constantly escaping, unobserved by the spectators, and is soaked up by the sand upon which the bowl rests. Thus, the experiment practically works itself, as soon as the water in the bowl falls enough to admit air to the cocoanut. All the magician has to do is to experiment, to find out the lapse of time between successive spoutings, and issue his commands accordingly.

Enchanted Crayons

Vanishing Knife

Magical Pistol and Card

● THE "Enchanted Crayons" is an excellent impromptu pocket trick, requiring no specially prepared apparatus. The conjurer simply provides himself with an unprepared box of different colored crayons, and a small metal tube, large enough to loosely hold one of the crayons. A metal cap for the tube, or container, is also necessary; the tube is permanently closed at the other end.

During the wizard's absence from the room, a spectator is requested to remove a crayon, and secrete it in the tube. After the cap has been placed upon the free end, the wizard is recalled to the room, and the closed tube handed to him, while his back is turned. After a moment or two of apparent concentration, the magician brings the tube from behind his back, and holds it to his forehead, immediately calling the color of the crayon concealed. The experiment may be repeated as often as desired, yet the wizard is always successful.

The explanation is as simple as the trick is mystifying. While holding the tube behind his back, the magician secretly removes the cap, permitting the crayon to slide a short distance out of the tube, and makes a mark therewith, upon his thumbnail, or runs the back of his fingernail against the crayon. The crayon then is replaced, as well as the cap. In the act of holding the tube before his forehead, the operator is naturally granted a momentary glance at the mark upon his thumbnail; thus enabling him to call the color of the crayon.

COLORED CRAYONS SUPER QUALITY

CAP

3/8"

CRAYON IN BRASS TUBE →

RED

3 3/4"

SCRATCH OF CRAYON ON THUMB NAIL

"X-ray vision" is demonstrated in the trick illustrated above. Crayon on the thumb gives the performer his cue.

An all-metal silver-plated table knife, of any common pattern, is visibly displayed, likewise a square of newspaper. Without any false or cumbersome moves, the knife is rolled inside the paper, permitting part of the blade to project, further to assure the audience that the knife is actually inside the parcel. The magician holds the package in his outstretched hand, and strikes the knife upon the back of a chair, proving by the sound that it is truly made of solid metal.

With sleeves turned up to the elbows, and with outstretched hands, he carefully pushes the blade inside the package, completely concealing the knife from view. A moment later, the paper is completely crushed between the palms of his hands, and rolled into a small ball, which is carelessly tossed aside,—the knife has completely vanished.

To prepare for this experiment, our

This simple arrangement permits a knife to be rolled into a newspaper, and vanish before the eyes.

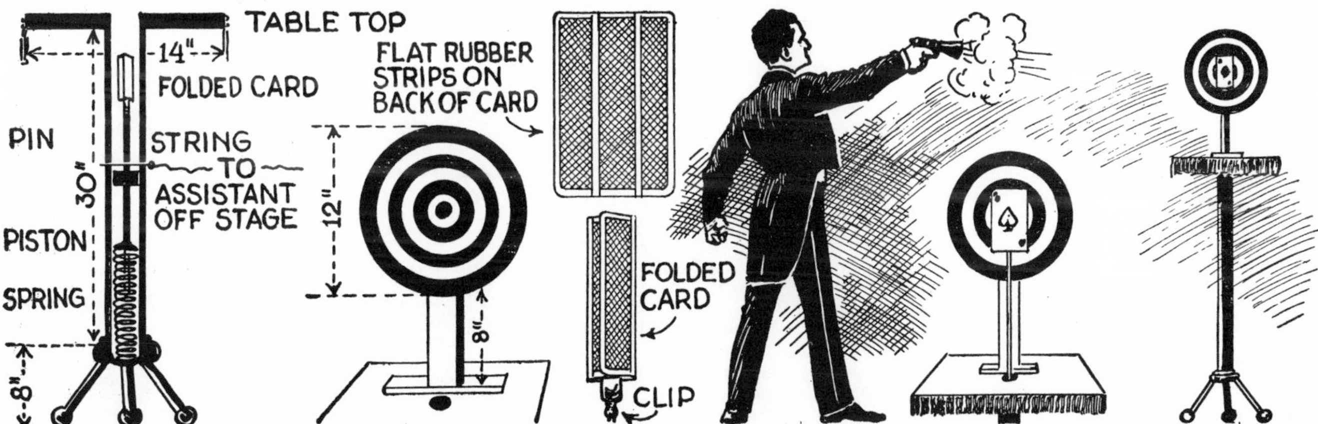

A card is torn, loaded into a pistol, and the "pieces" fired at an unprepared target, where the card appears seemingly restored again. The mechanical stand makes the illusion possible, as the details illustrate.

magical mechanic constructs a small pocket, large enough to fit over the knife-blade, from a piece of silver paper. At a short distance, this pocket will look exactly like the knife-blade proper, and will appear quite real.

In the act of striking the knife upon the back of a chair, the wizard secretly permits the knife itself to slide out through the lower end of the paper parcel, into a small bag, affixed secretly to the back of a chair.

The silvered paper slide remains in view, leading the audience to believe that the knife is still inside the paper, long after it has been actually disposed of. The rest is naturally easy.

Mechanical card tricks have been a favorite, with both professional and amateur magicians, for a great number of years. The one herewith described, is sensational in effect, outstanding in mystery, and yet easily constructed. A wooden target of the dimensions illustrated, is passed for inspection, and is found unprepared. The wizard then places it upon a small side stand. A card, selected by one of the audience, is torn to pieces, which are then placed into the funnel-tube attachment of the magician's pistol. Standing at some distance from the target, and aiming toward it, the wizard fires; and the playing card is found completely restored, and mysteriously attached to the center of the target. Now for the secret:

The card is *forced* upon the spectator. If the amateur is not sufficiently dexterous to force a card, he may use a deck composed of fifty-two cards, of one suit and denomination—in other words, all alike. Thus *any* card chosen will be the proper one. A duplicate of this card is concealed and attached to a piston, working inside the leg of the side stand, as illustrated. This is held in place by means of a common pin, tied to a fine silk thread, the free end of which is in the hands of an offstage assistant. At the pistol's report, the string is pulled, and the card is driven upward, and in front of the target, by the piston, which is attached to a spiral spring, and shoots the card rapidly into position. The playing card has previously been cut into three sections, to the backs of which have been glued two narrow strips of elastic, or flat rubber. These cause the card to expand, when making its appearance; thereby opening out the face to its full extent.

Mystic Wine Production

Magical Marksmanship

The Magnetized Knife

● IN the mystic production of wine effect, a 16″ square of cartridge paper is passed for inspection; and finally returned to the magician, who forms it into a cone. With a scissors, the magician cuts off the tip at the end of the cone, and a large quantity of wine is seen to flow into a transparent glass container, held beneath the cone. The paper is then rolled into a ball and tossed aside.

The wizard is secretly provided with a flexible rubber container, about 2″ in diameter, and 12″ long, as illustrated. This "sausage" is filled with wine, and the end of the container tied or corked; it is then concealed in the performer's sleeve. After the paper cone has been formed, the magician secretly permits the wine container to slide out of his sleeve, and into the cone. This act is easily concealed in the move of reaching for the glass goblet (which later is to contain the wine). When the magician cuts away the end of the cone, he secretly removes the cork; which naturally allows the wine to flow. Being flexible, the rubber tube, now empty, is easily crushed, together with the paper cone, rolled into a ball, and tossed aside.

Wine apparently flows from an empty paper cone.

The effect to be desired next is appropriately named "Magical Marksmanship." A deck of cards is exhibited, and the ace of spades is removed. The performer's eyes are securely blindfolded, by a committee of several spectators. Standing at the opposite side of the stage, an assistant holds the playing card at arm's length. The blindfolded wizard fires a single shot from a pistol, in the direction of the playing card. Upon examination, it is found that the conjurer has apparently shot a hole exactly in the center of the card.

The shot fired from the pistol comes from a blank cartridge. The playing card is a mechanical one, prepared as illustrated; it consists of two cards, glued together around the edges, through both of which a hole has been previously pierced. A small section cut from a third playing card, operates upon a pivot, between the two cards. Thus, the assistant has simply to move the protruding projection, to cause this strip to move away from its original position, and thus show the perforation through the center of the card. If the magician desires to elaborate upon this effect, he might afterward secretly exchange the mechanical card for a duplicate and unprepared ace of spades, through which a hole had been punched.

This will, of course, permit a close inspection of the card, after the presentation of the effect.

Although his eyes are securely blindfolded, the magician is able to shoot a hole clean through the center of the ace of spades. Of course it is a trick; the method of operation is given in the text.

Our last effect, this month, is the magnetized knife.

A common and unprepared table knife is passed for inspection. The magician, with arms bare to the elbow, apparently makes several hypnotic passes over the knife, when it is seen to adhere mysteriously to the magician's palm, defying all accepted

Table knife hangs from the palm, because of the unseen hair.

laws of gravitation. At the wizard's command, the magnetic spell is broken, and the knife is at once passed for reinspection. The conjurer's fingers are likewise examined, and are found to be completely unprepared.

A small loop of human hair is responsible for this startling effect. It is originally carried around the thumb, and is secretly looped over the end of the knife, where it rests in position, so that the loop is imbedded in the groove between the handle and the blade of the knife. A light pressure of the thumb, against the edge of the blade, causes the knife to remain mystically suspended. The hair is dropped to the floor, before the knife and fingers are afterward examined.

Vanishing Bird and Cage

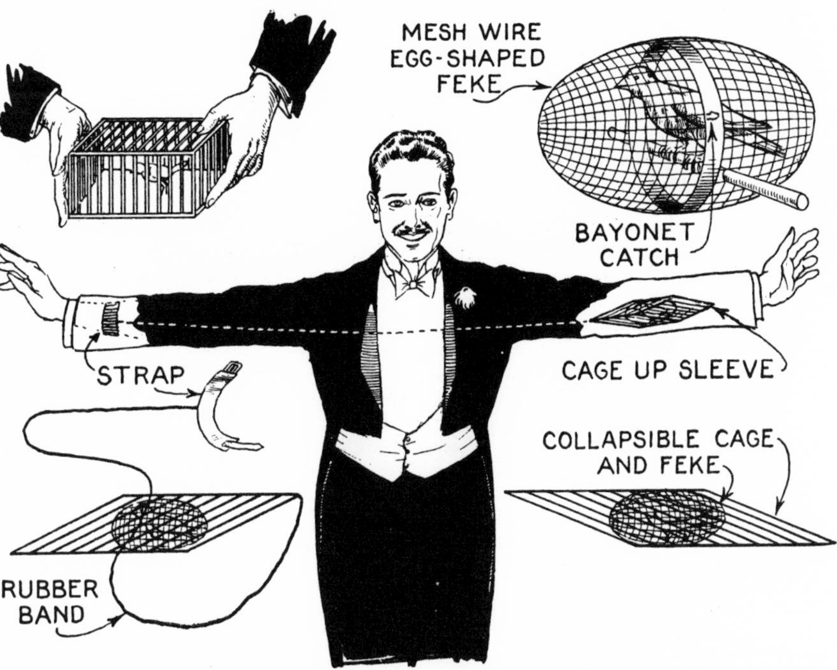

THE DeKolta vanishing bird cage has of late become quite a common feature in the programs of many wonder workers throughout the nation. The effect consists of carrying forth a small cage, containing a living canary, between the magician's palms. At the mystic count of three, the cage is apparently tossed into mid-air, and completely vanishes with a lightning rapidity. The trick consists of a collapsible cage, built with all joints of the wires movable, so as to enable the cage and its feathered occupant to make its way into the magician's sleeve. It is thus carried out of sight, being attached to a strap and sash cord arrangement, the cord leading from the wrist of the left arm, clear around the magician's back, and down the right sleeve through the armhole, where it is attached to a corner of the cage. Unfortunately, nine times in ten, the bird is an innocent victim of circumstances, and is either killed or badly injured during its disappearance.

The author's improvement consists of having the bird encased in a small egg-shaped feke, composed of a wire mesh, of light wire, as illustrated. This feke, which opens up so that the bird may be placed in or taken out of it, is attached to the perch of the cage. My readers will readily conceive that in the act of the cage collapsing, the wires can in no way come in direct contact with the bird, and therefore saves him from becoming a tom-cat's banquet. If the wires of the feke are very thin, they will not be seen at the usual spectator's distance, as they are hidden by the cage wires.

How Did the Screw Get There?

● HERE is a unique and startling mystery, which is sure to create considerable comment. As will be observed in the diagram below, a long wood-screw is driven through a wooden rod which is (apparently) a continuation of the stopper of the bottle. This cork may be lifted from the bottle and worked up until the screw catches against the neck or narrowing sides. The article then becomes a still greater mystery.

By way of construction, note cut-away diagram at the right. It will be observed that the wooden extension of the cork or top of the bottle is made from the same material, but the rod itself has been thread-fitted into the stopper. A hole is drilled through this rod, three-quarters of the way down, and then another hole is drilled transversely through the rod; this should be large enough to accommodate the screw. A bottle is obtained and the screw measured so that it, together with the wooden peg, will be approximately the same length as the diameter of the bottle.

The cut-away diagram shows the manner in which this puzzling novelty is constructed.

A piece of thread is now passed through the hole in the peg and permitted to come out through the transverse opening. This is then tied to the exact middle of the screw, brought out toward the end, and here the thread is tipped to the point of the screw with a bit of glue which is allowed to harden. When ready for the assembly, the peg is held between the fingers at an angle, the screw dropped into the bottle, and the thread pulled until the point of the screw enters the transverse opening. A sharp tug on the thread will now free it from its glued attachment, and the screw can be wiggled into its final resting place. A piece of iron wire is dropped into the vertical hole of the peg until it contacts with the screw and, when the stopper is pulled up tight against the peg, the wire serves to grip the screw in place firmly.

Unstainable Paper

The Enchanted Jug

Living and Dead Trick

Adding more "ink" from the bottle destroys the blackening property of the ink in the well.

● A PIECE of white paper, previously examined and found unprepared, is rolled up into a cylinder and plunged into the contents of an ink well. When withdrawn it is naturally covered with ink. The stained paper is placed upon a plate and passed about as evidence to prove that the well really contains ink.

To replace the ink thus removed, the magician fills the ink well from an ordinary bottle of ink, and the experiment with the paper is repeated. On this occasion, however, much to the amazement of the spectators, the paper comes out as white as when it went in. It may be passed for immediate inspection.

Explanation: The ink well is really full of ink, but the bottle from which the new supply was supposedly obtained, does not contain ink, but finely powdered resin instead. In the act of (apparently) refilling the ink well, the magician secretly sprinkles the surface of the ink with this finely powdered substance which prevents the ink from touching the paper. Upon removing the paper, a slight shake will disengage any powder clinging to it. Lycopodium powder could also be used instead of the resin.

The next effect is an entirely new method for presenting the ever popular "living and dead" trick; quite a sensational item upon the average magician's program.

The effect is as follows: the wizard passes out eight or nine small squares of paper to various members of the audience and, offering a pencil to the first one, requests that the name of some departed person, known only to the spectator, be written upon the slip. Without divulging the name to anybody, the paper is folded, concealing the writing.

This enchanted jug apparently clings to ordinary rope dropped into the mouth; the ball does it.

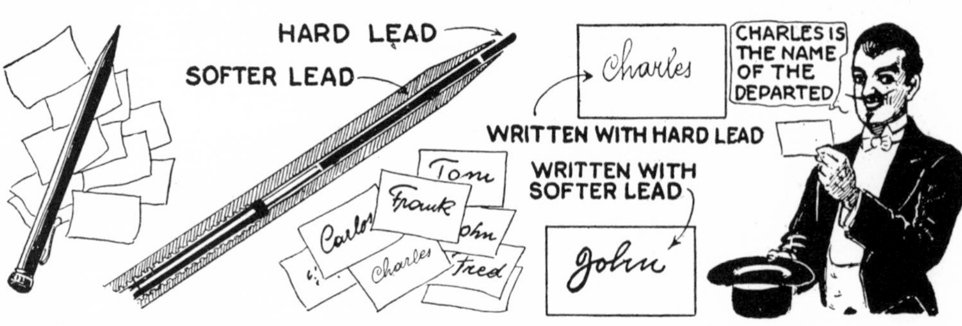

On identical slips are written the names of one departed person and others alive. The performer has no difficulty in discovering the name of the deceased, the lead tells the story.

OOOOOOOOOOOOOOOOOOOOOOOOO

In succession, the pencil is next passed to the remaining spectators, with a request that each also write one name upon individual slips, but all these names are to be those of persons still living. These papers are also folded in like manner, and all the slips deposited into a borrowed hat; or, if the entertainer chooses, they may be placed upon a platter.

The conjuror now opens one paper after the other, reading each paper aloud as he does so. At each reading he pretends to consult some invisible spirit who he explains, whispers to him whether or not the name called is that of one still on the earth plane, or a departed spirit. Strangely enough, the wizard is able through some seemingly mysterious force, to correctly identify the name of the departed one.

The explanation of this startling effect is as simple as it is mysterious. The pencil which the wizard has handed out, as a convenience to the persons who do the writing, is of the mechanical variety now commonly sold in every stationery shop.

This pencil had previously been loaded in the usual manner with a length of soft lead, on top of which a very short piece of hard lead has been planted. Thus the first name written, (the name of a person departed) was written with hard lead.

In the act of passing the pencil to the next person, a slight twist of the pencil forces the short length of lead out of the barrel, dropping it secretly to the floor. This brings the soft lead into proper position for writing the names upon the rest of the slips. The reader will, therefore, note that, as all the remaining names are of living persons, they can easily be distinguished from the first one; since the writing was done with a different quality of lead.

The Enchanted Jug is a small earthen jug of Mexican variety, purchasable in the average Mexican novelty shop. The jug is approximately eight inches high and has a mouth about 1¼" in diameter. This, together with a length of rope about a yard long, of soft texture, is passed for examination. The articles, being found intact, are returned to the magician; he drops end of the rope into the mouth of the jug, as illustrated. After uttering a mystic oriental chant, the rope is slowly raised into the air and the jug, leaving the level of the table, mysteriously clings to the rope as though magnetized.

Explanation: A small rubber ball, which has been secretly palmed, is introduced into the jug, and, by manipulating the jug while talking to the audience, it is rolled into a position where it becomes a wedge between the inner wall of the jug and the rope. (The method is clearly illustrated). After a presentation of the illusion a slight tap on the base of the jug will cause the ball to drop from its wedged position, thereby releasing the rope. The ball is permitted to roll out of the jug into the magician's palm where it is again secreted, and disposed of; permitting both rope and jug to be reexamined.

Psychomotrized Ashes

Indian Snake Materialization

The Fishy Fishbowl

● THE first effect described here is, unquestionably, one of the simplest and most effective for secretly obtaining information, written upon a card, previously sealed securely in an envelope. The effect of its presentation consists of requesting a subject to write a sentence, a series of names, a date of birth, or similar subject, upon a small card, which he is requested to seal inside an unprepared envelope. The magician collects the envelope, and together with its contents, burns it. The ashes are permitted to drop upon a common china plate; and the psychic, with an utterance of the mystic abracadabra, proceeds to "psychomotrize" the ashes. Mysteriously enough, he reads aloud the name or message, which was originally written upon the visiting card.

Explanation: The magician has provided himself with the ever-useful false thumb (made of aluminum or other thin material, painted flesh color and fitting the natural thumb, like a thimble). To this has been affixed the corner of a sharp razor blade. In the act of returning to the platform, with the envelope in his hand, the performer secretly cuts a section of the envelope, enabling him to read what has been written upon the card, as shown in the illustration. In the act of lighting the envelope, ample time is provided for him to read the message.

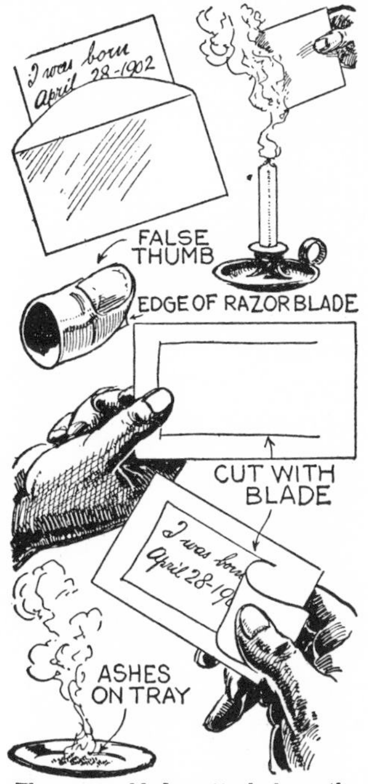

The razor blade, attached to the false thumb, enables the magician to cut the envelope in such a fashion that its contents will be disclosed.

Covering an empty fish bowl with a cloth mysteriously fills the contents of the bowl.

India, the home of mystery, again supplies an astounding and heretofore unexplained illusion, with which street fakirs have mystified and bewildered the unsuspecting tourists. The dark-skinned necromancer requests a spectator to fill both hands with sand from the ground. With an unsuspected gesture, and after several moments devoted to the uttering of mystic chants, the magician suddenly strikes the hands of the spectator a sharp blow, causing the sand to be spilled upon the ground. As the dust cloud, produced by this action, subsides, several snakes and small reptiles are seen crawling upon the ground which, a moment before, was unquestionably vacant.

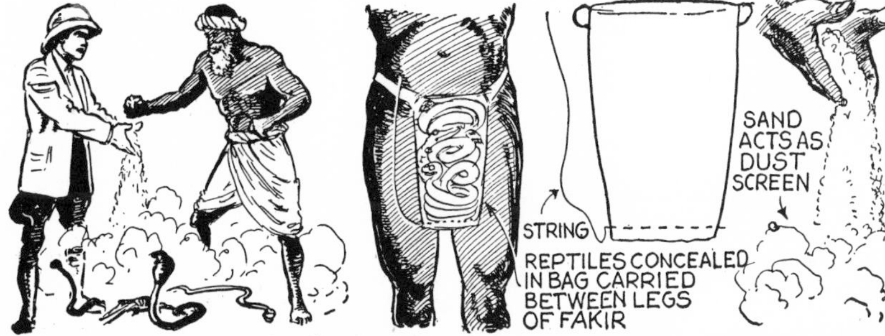

Under cover of a screen of falling dust, the necromancer can produce a quantity of snakes. The bag, suspended from the waist, and its ingenious release is responsible for the effect.

Explanation: The reptiles are concealed in a small bag, suspended from the waist of the fakir, as illustrated. A string, sewed through the open end of the bag, retains the "load" till the proper time when the string is secretly pulled, permitting the reptiles to drop to the ground. The cloud of dust, produced by the sand, naturally acts as a "smoke screen" to conceal the action. The fakir is usually nude, save for the traditional loin cloth, worn about his waist, which is sufficient to conceal the "load."

For the third effect, we present a fish story. A transparent glass fish bowl is passed for inspection, and then partly filled with water and placed in full view upon an undraped table. A black silk cloth, about 24″ square, is inspected, and thrown across the back of a chair, while the magician rolls up his sleeves. The black cloth is, for a moment, used as a cover for the bowl and, upon removing it, a dozen or more large goldfish are discovered swimming about in the water.

Explanation: The fish are contained in a closely-woven hairnet, made of very fine silk, and sewn in bag fashion, with a thin wire hook attached; this bag of fish is originally concealed inside a waterholder, attached to the back of a chair. Before the rolling up of the sleeves, the cloth is casually placed across the back of the chair. When it is again lifted, the "load" of fish is secretly carried beneath it, and deposited inside the fish bowl, in the act of covering it. The spectators, if seated at a short distance from the bowl, will be quite unable to see the almost invisible hairnet bag.

Rabbit From Hat — The Standing Matchbook — The Writing Blackboard

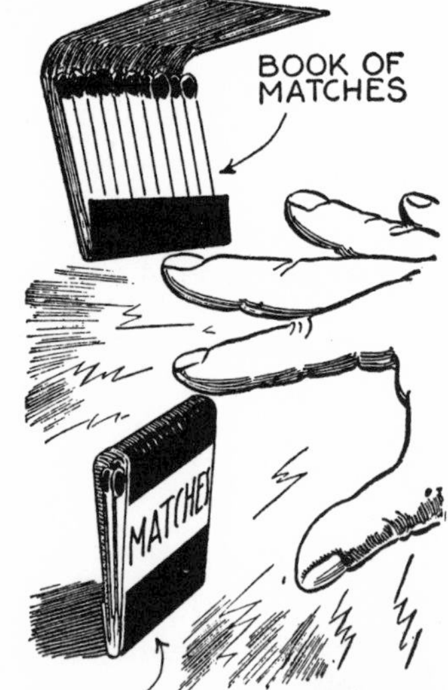

● THE first effect illustrated this month is a new and original method for loading a hat. The magician passes for inspection an opera hat, which is found quite unprepared, and is then opened and placed on top of a small table or side stand. A silk foulard or large handkerchief, which has been likewise examined, is used to cover the hat for a few moments, during which some mysterious passes are made.

Upon removing the foulard, the magician, with arms bared to the elbow, reaches inside the hat, and pulls forth a large live rabbit and, if desired, he likewise produces a number of flags, colored silks, ribbons, etc. The illustration clearly shows how an assistant, concealed in the wings, operates a long pole to which has been tied a strong black string; the free end of the latter has been secretly tied to the load packed into a small black bag, and placed upon the servante (a shelf in back of the table).

In the act of placing the silk over the hat, it is held up (as illustrated) for a moment during which the concealed assistant, by manipulating the stick, secretly lifts the load from behind the table, permitting the performer to swing it inside the hat under cover of the handkerchief, which conceals the entire action from the audience.

An ingenious method of getting a load into a hat, without manipulating the hat.

Here is an excellent trick for the parlor magician. An ordinary paper of matches, of the paper-packet variety, now quite commonly used, is displayed. These may be his own or, if desired, borrowed from a spectator. Standing the case on edge on the table, the conjurer removes his hand; the case is found to remain standing mysteriously upon its edge without any visible means of support. Explanation: One match is secretly bent over the lower edge of the case, and the cover replaced, as illustrated. This acts as a support for the case when it is stood upon its edge. The match is, of course, replaced to its proper position when the matches are passed for inspection after the presentation of the trick.

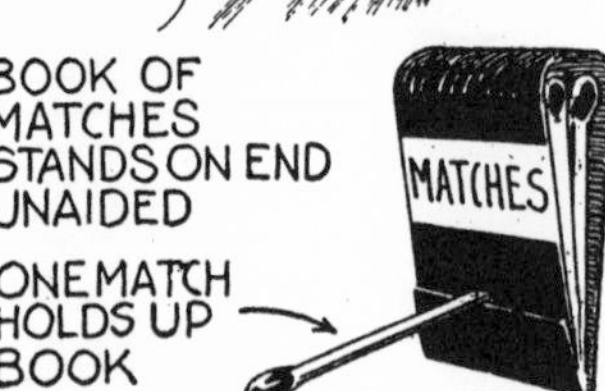

When prepared as shown, a book of matches stands on end.

The writer will now explain a sensational and mystifying illusion which has for years bewildered thousands of spectators who have witnessed its presentation, both in the United States and abroad. A huge blackboard is seen resting upon a substantially constructed easel, the legs of which elevate the blackboard well above the level of the stage. The conjurer removes a piece of chalk from an ordinary chalk box, and holds it against the surface of the slate, to which it mysteriously adheres. A name is chosen by someone in the audience, and is called aloud for all to hear. Standing at a distance from the apparatus, the magician makes a few mysterious passes when, much to the amazement of the audience, the apparently magnetized piece of chalk begins to move slowly over the surface of the blackboard, and spells out letter by letter, the name previously called.

Secret: A small boy (in some instances a midget) is concealed behind the blackboard and operates a strong magnet, by which he moves the chalk over the surface of the board. (Concealed in the piece of chalk is a piece of steel.) Some performers prefer to show the blackboard after the illusion has been presented; by removing it from the easel, and displaying it from all sides. In this case, the boy first makes his getaway through a small opening in the back of the scenery.

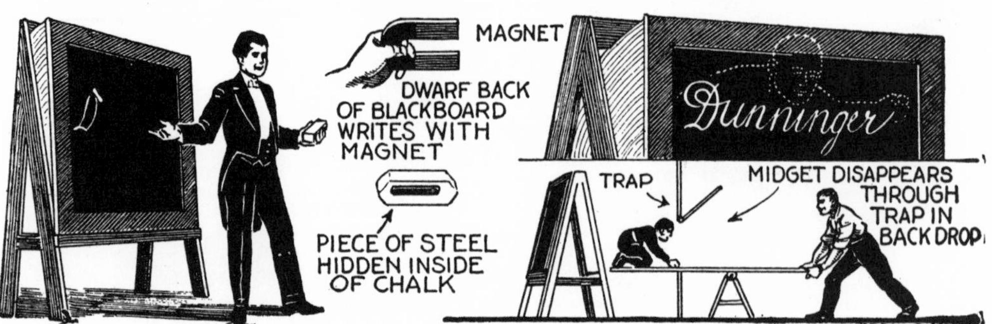

A piece of chalk writes upon the blackboard any name called. It is manipulated from behind board as illustrated.

The Balancing Glass — Bullet Catching — The Severed Thread

● IN the *Balancing Glass* trick, the first presented this month, we have an original improvement upon a universally-known after-dinner experiment, which is a most mystifying effect. A drinking glass, half full of liquid, is placed upon the dinner table at an angle, and, after a minute or two of dexterous balancing, the wizard removes his fingers, and the glass is seen to remain standing upon its edge, mystically balanced at an almost impossible angle.

Before presenting this effect, the magician has secretly placed a wooden matchstick (of the square variety, with head broken off) beneath the tablecloth. This acts as a wedge, against which the edge of the glass rests. The writer's improvement consists of a fine silk thread tied to the end of the match; the free end of the thread hangs beneath the tablecloth. After presenting the trick, one can easily pull the match away from beneath the cloth, permitting it to drop to the floor. This action can easily be executed without detection, while the wizard is still seated at the table, doing the trick. Thus, many who know the old method, will be doubly mystified when they look beneath the cloth and find no matchstick there.

For years, bogus "spiritualistic mediums" have attempted to create effects with which to mystify and thus convince their audience. It has been a generally accepted fact that, when a medium succeeded in astounding a group with some unexplainable effect or illusion, the spectators simply credited the medium with spiritual or supernatural powers, rather than believe they had been subjected to a deception beyond their own mental powers of analysis.

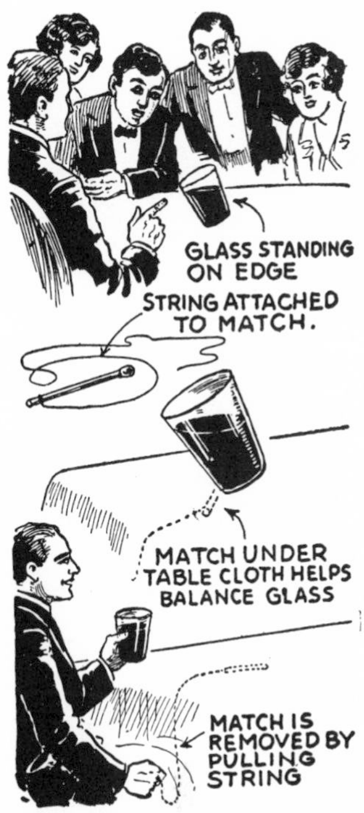

A glass can be balanced against a square match; which then is removed by pulling the thread.

COVER
GLASS JAR
SILK THREAD
SEALING WAX
MATCHES
TAPE
SILK FASTENED TO BOTTOM WITH AID OF STICK
SUNLIGHT BURNS SILK

Ostensibly a "spirit" trick; the conjuror can "break" the thread in the bottle with a magnifying glass as shown.

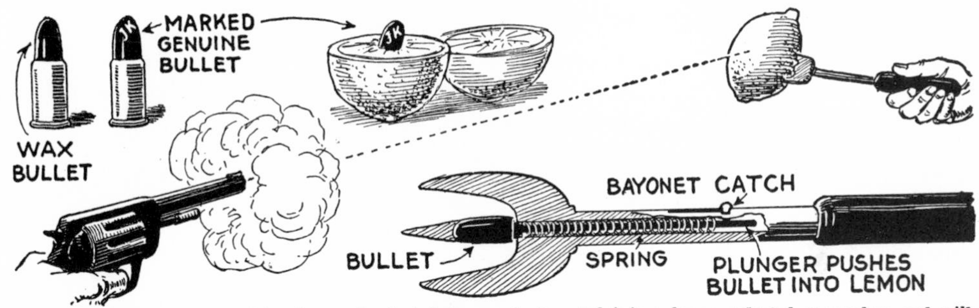

A marked bullet, mounted in the mechanical fork, can be inserted into a lemon selected at random and will be found there at the end of the demonstration.

An American medium of international reputation recently presented a somewhat new effect, with which he mystified a great many groups as well as a number of magicians. Here is my method of duplicating his effect. The presentation consists of having the end of a thread fastened to the bottom of a glass jar, with some sealing wax. The free end of the thread runs upwards and through a small hole in the cover of the jar, which should be of the screwtop variety. This end of the thread, after being drawn taut, is firmly held in place with more sealing wax; after which various strips of tape, wound around the top, and also sealed and marked, are used to make it quite impossible for anyone to tinker with the affair without breaking the seals or otherwise leaving proof of tampering. The medium, after retiring with the jar into another room, returns to his group of sitters who find, upon examination, the silk thread cut clear through the center; the seals are unbroken, and the jar otherwise intact. The medium naturally claims that the phenomenon has been produced by spirits; as the application of any earthly agency would be quite impossible under the circumstances.

To throw light upon the subject (in fact, SUN light upon the subject) it will be found that, by using a strong magnifying glass, the rays of the sun can be focussed upon the thread, and in a short time will burn it through. The glass of the jar does not stop rays of heat, any more than it does those of light.

In the *Bullet Catching* trick, we present a new and startling effect by using a new piece of apparatus. A gentleman (chosen by a committee of spectators from the audience) is asked to step upon the stage and assist the magician; by selecting a lemon, which he chooses at random from eighteen or twenty contained in a basket. The magician requests a second spectator to remove a bullet from a box, containing a gross or more. This bullet is marked and then placed in a gun, which is left with this spectator. The wizard returns to the stage; places the selected lemon upon a fork which he holds; and requests the assistant spectator, in the audience, to take aim in the direction of the lemon and fire. The lemon is now removed from the fork, and the fruit cut in two, with a borrowed penknife; much to the amazement of the spectators, the marked bullet is discovered imbedded inside the lemon!

The fork employed is a mechanical one, construction of which is made clear by the diagram. A small piston, operated upon a spring, and controlled by a bayonet catch, forces the concealed bullet through a small opening into the fruit. The mechanical side of the fork is held away from the audience when presenting the trick. While among the spectators, the magician has exchanged the marked bullet for a wax bullet, which was loaded into the gun, instead of the original. Returning to the stage, the conjurer secretly dropped the marked bullet inside the basket containing the remaining lemons, and an assistant nonchalantly carried the basket off stage. Concealed in the wings, the assistant quickly removed the marked bullet from the cartridge with a pair of pliers, and secreted it in the mechanical fork, which was then carried to the stage and handed to the conjurer. The wizard has but to insert the fork into the lemon, and secretly release the bayonet catch; thereby forcing the bullet into position inside the fruit. The rest of the trick is a matter of showmanship.

Disappearing Cigarettes Vanishing Tumbler Fakir Sword Penetration

● CIGARETTE tricks are quite the vogue, as no doubt has been noted by the many readers who have lately attended variety or vaudeville performances. The experiment herein described is one of the most astounding, and seemingly difficult, of all cigarette tricks. Although it seems to be an effect which requires years of practice to perfect, it is in reality exceedingly simple to operate. The magician forms his left hand into a fist. Four spectators are requested to light cigarettes, which are handed to the wizard, one after the other. As he receives them, he places them, lighted ends down, into his closed fist. On slowly opening his fingers, all four cigarettes are found to have mystically disappeared.

Explanation: A specially constructed "feke," in the form of a metal pull, is responsible for the disappearance. The pull is attached, as illustrated, to a strong piece of elastic, which carries it up the sleeve, and out of sight. It is divided into four compartments, each one of which holds a cigarette firmly and, as the burning end enters the metal holder, the cigarette is automatically extinguished. The fact that four cigarettes are vanished, at one and the same time, is a decided improvement over the old cigarette-vanishing pull, which was constructed for the disappearance of but one lit cigarette.

In the vanishing tumbler effect, the magician brings forth a large glass tumbler, containing a beverage which he drinks. After the glass has been emptied of its contents, it is placed, mouth down, upon a table top. A cone is now made from a sheet of newspaper and, holding the cone in one hand, the glass is removed from the table, and placed inside the cone. Without suspicious moves, and with arms bare to the elbow, the magician crushes the cone between his fingers, rolls it into a small ball, and carelessly tosses it aside. The glass has completely vanished.

Explanation: A cone, constructed of heavy cellophane, fits loosely over the glass tumbler. In the act of picking up the glass, the tumbler is secretly dropped into a bag supported upon a wire frame, which has been attached to the back of the table. Thus, the cellophane cone, (which in reality appears to be the tumbler), is slowly lowered into the mouth of the paper cone and, a moment later, is crushed between the performer's hands, and tossed aside.

Many are the tales of magic and mystery which come from the East. Reports recently arrived of a new mystery, in which the faker parades the streets of Calcutta, with a long, twenty-inch dagger, penetrating his cheeks. When a few coppers are dropped into his ever-open palm, he nonchalantly opens his mouth, displaying the remainder of the blade, which is clearly seen.

Explanation: In spite of the faker's spiritual countenance, the affair is but a clever deception. As illustrated, the dagger is of special construction. The two sections of the blade are held close to his cheeks, by a concealed metal loop, easily kept from view by his thick full-grown beard. A special piece of steel, constructed with two loops, is held between his jaws, and helps to complete the illusion when his mouth is opened wide.

Disappearing an empty tumbler by a cellophane substitute.

FOUR CIGARETTES STUCK INTO FIST WITH LIGHTED END DOWN

FEKE DISAPPEARS UP THE SLEEVE

FEKE

ELASTIC

FOUR OPENINGS

With the feke here illustrated, four cigarettes may be vanished at a time.

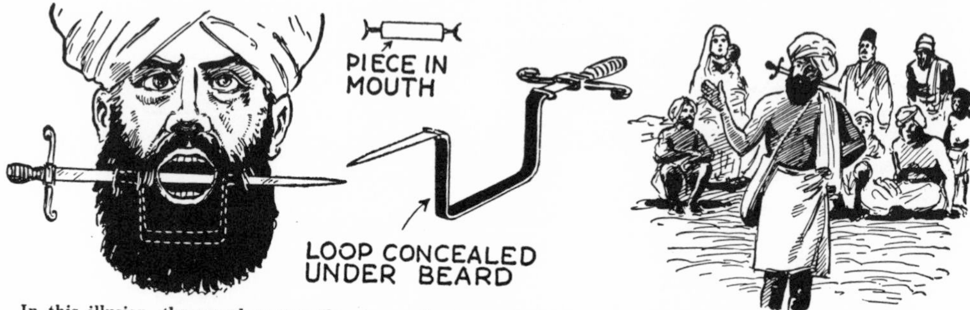

In this illusion, the sword apparently pierces the jaws of the mystic; when he opens his mouth, the blade may be seen inside. Actually, the blade is made in two parts, as shown.

Chinese Coin Divination
Pitcher of Plenty
Indian Horn Blowing Trick

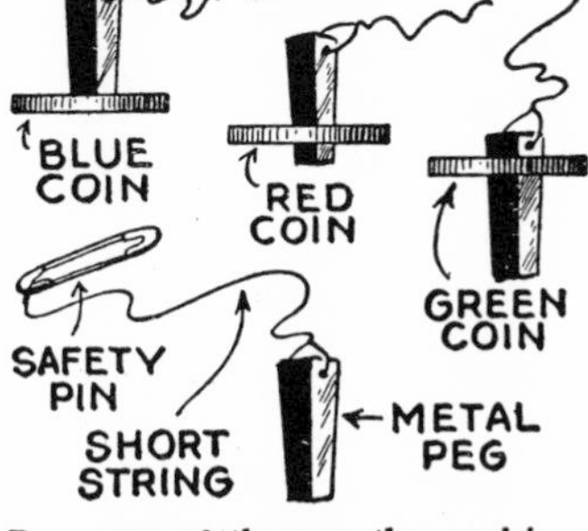

By means of the peg, the magician is able to tell the color of the coin, even though he is blindfolded.

● THIS month, we present a divination trick — always an interesting experiment in magical demonstrations — since pocket tricks easily performed and startling in effect, are always desirable this one is described. Three Chinese coins, painted respectively in the colors green, red and blue, are passed for minute inspection, and are apparently unprepared. Any one of these may be handed to the conjurer who, with his hands held behind his back, successfully names the color thereof. The experiment may be repeated as often as desired.

Concealed beneath the magician's coat is a small, slightly tapered piece of metal, fixed to a short string, the free end of which is tied to a safety pin. The holes in the center of the coins vary slightly; so that, by inserting the metal peg into the hole, the magician is able to divine the color of the coin which he is holding. It is impossible for the eye to discern any difference in the size of the holes—therefore the trick is practically foolproof.

A mystery, reported to have been presented by a Hindu fakir, consisted of a demonstration in which he sounded a horn by placing the mouth of the instrument upon the skin of the neck. As it is our purpose to explain mysteries which have not been heretofore exposed, we are describing this startling effect for readers of SCIENCE AND MECHANICS.

The secret is as simple as it is mysterious. Concealed beneath the robe, which the fakir wore, was a duplicate horn, held in place by a strap encircling his body, as illustrated. A rubber ball, attached to the mouth of the trumpet, was located beneath his armpit. A slight amount of pressure forced the air

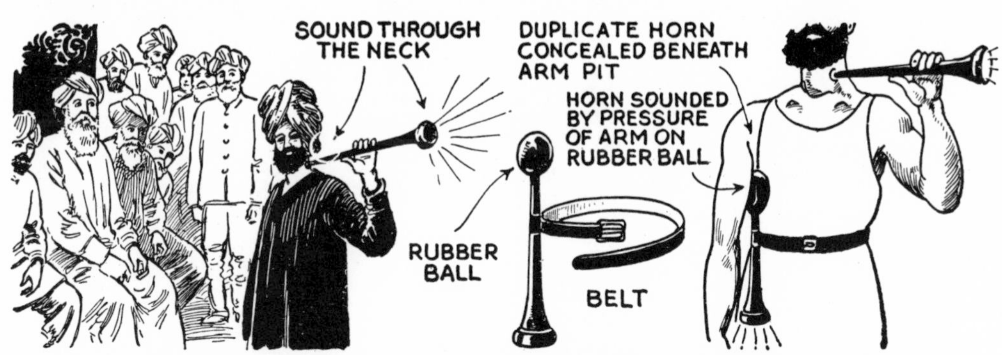

In the effect above illustrated, a horn is apparently sounded through the neck. Actually, a duplicate horn is strapped to the waist, with its rubber ball located under the armpit, and sounded by applying pressure to the ball, but spectators think it is the horn at the throat.

Dividing the contents of a pitcher by layers of paraffin permits a spectacular demonstration. All of the products are genuine and may be tasted by the spectators.

through the instrument, producing the sounds which, apparently, came from the displayed trumpet.

The *Pitcher of Plenty* is a new and original effect, quite simple to present, and by far one of the most effective deceptions in the realm of present-day conjuring. A metal pitcher, with a swingback sieve attachment affixed (the type used for ice-water, to prevent the ice cubes from being poured out with the water), is standing upon the magician's table, together with drinking vessels of various types, such as water, wine, milk glasses, etc. The magician, his arms bared to the elbow, pours a glass or two of water out of the pitcher and, for a moment, stirs the remaining contents with a previously-examined wand (an unprepared dowel stick, twelve or fourteen inches long, will do). He now pours a further quantity of the pitcher's contents into the wine glasses, and the liquid proves to be real sherry. Some more stirring with the wand, and several glasses of milk are poured from the same pitcher. The spectators also partake of this, and attest to its genuineness. Once again, the wand stirs the remaining contents, and now the performer empties the pitcher into a bowl; this time the mystic production consisting of various colors of hard candies. The empty pitcher is then passed for inspection immediately and is found to be entirely unprepared.

To prepare for this trick, the magician has provided himself with several cakes of paraffin (parawax), which has been melted by heating and poured into a saucer. A quantity of candy is placed into the pitcher and covered by waxed paper; some paraffin is poured over it, and permitted to harden. Some milk is next poured into the pitcher, followed by another quantity of the liquid wax, which likewise clings to the inner walls of the pitcher, and hardens. The wine next, is followed by wax and the water last. As each of the liquids is produced, the wand is used to stir the contents, but secretly breaks the layers of wax. As the candy is produced after all the liquids have been poured out of the pitcher, the shattered bits of wax are emptied into the bowl with the candy and, at a short distance, look like pieces of real candy. The wizard, with a pair of tongs, removes a few pieces of clean candy, which he places upon a tray, and offers to the spectators. The sieve prevents the wax from being poured out with the various liquids, during presentation of the early stages of the mystery.

Enchanted Tablecloth Resurrected Thread Latticework Box

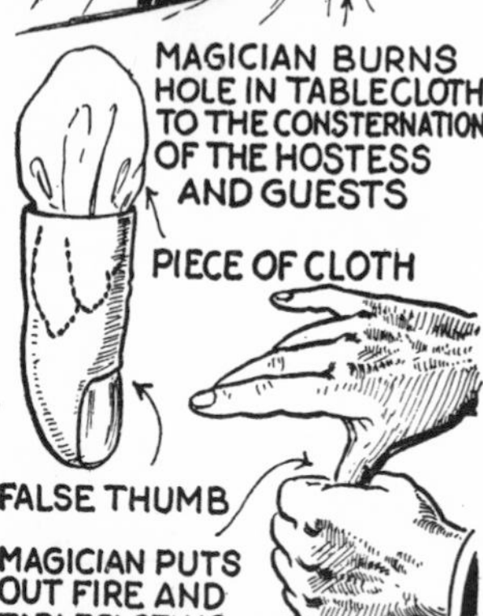

A surprising effect is this one in which a tablecloth is apparently burned and later restored.

● THE first effect to be described, in this issue, is the "Enchanted Tablecloth," a splendid impromptu trick, which you might try on your next visit to a friend's house. Bunch up the center of the tablecloth between your fingers and, striking a match, light the center of the cloth until it is aflame. After you have blown out the fire, you proceed to push the burnt edges of the blackened cloth slowly back into your hand. Then, upon releasing the cloth, it is found to be entirely intact, and no amount of examination will reveal any trace of the fabric's having ever been burned.

Explanation: The conjuror's reliable and ever useful "false thumb" is again necessary, but this time it plans an entirely new rôle in the conjuror's repertoire. The thumb is previously loaded with a small piece of cloth, which is pulled into view, and is actually set aflame; but the audience believes it to be the center of the tablecloth. After the fire has been extinguished, the remains of the cloth are again pushed inside the false thumb but, to the spectators, it simply seems that the cloth is being forced back inside the wizard's closed fist. The false thumb with its contents secretly remains, of course, upon the magician's thumb; enabling him to show his hands completely empty, and the cloth apparently restored. The false thumb is, of course, flesh-colored.

For the second effect, the wizard displays a latticework transparent box, the front edge of which is hinged to skeleton-frame tabouret. The box, which is bottomless, is tipped, permitting the spectators to look through it and is then replaced into its original position; whereupon the magician proceeds to spin the entire apparatus completely around, displaying all its sides freely. Although the box seems entirely empty, the conjurer, with elbows bared, places his hands inside the box, and proceeds to draw forth a large number of silk flags, handkerchiefs, live flowers (which are distributed to the audience) and a goodly number of pigeons, rabbits, a duck, and other appropriate livestock.

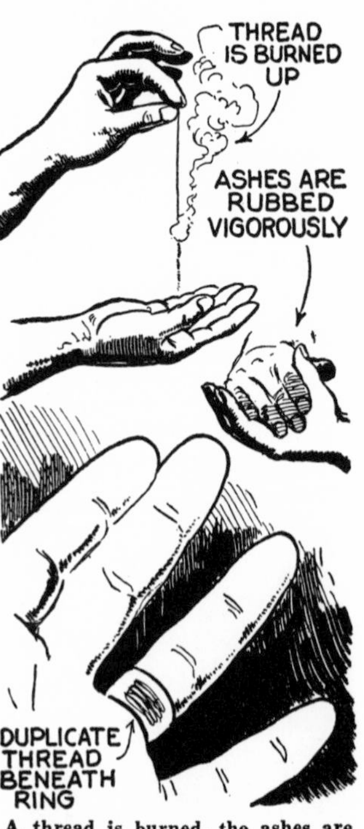

A thread is burned, the ashes are collected, and the thread is again restored by the method here illustrated.

A bottomless box, transparent except for a lattice-like effect, serves for the production of volumes of silk, flowers, and even live animals. The secret lies within the pedestal.

Explanation: The diagram plainly shows the dimensions of the box and tabouret, and also clearly illustrates, a cleverly-hidden container in which the load, tightly packed, has been previously concealed. A zipper, sewed to the center of two cloth flaps, holds the load in place until the time of its production. At a short distance, it is impossible to suspect that the quantity of articles produced could possibly be concealed in the apparatus.

Another excellent impromptu trick is the "Resurrected Thread" effect. The magician's arms are bared to the elbows, his hands appearing quite empty. Taking a spool of thread, he breaks off a piece about a yard long. Holding one end of the thread in outstretched hand, he requests a spectator to ignite the free end of the thread with a match; and the thread is seen to burn completely. The magician permits the ashes to drop into the palm of his other hand, which has been held beneath the burning thread. After he rubs his hands together for a moment or two, the thread is found completely restored, and is opened out to its full length, much to the mystification of the spectators.

Explanation: A duplicate piece of thread, of length equal to the one destroyed, has been folded into a small parcel, and has been previously concealed beneath the magician's finger ring. As most gentlemen wear rings, this is not suspected when the wizard bares his arms to the elbows, and displays his hands apparently empty. The rubbing his hands briskly together before bringing the duplicate thread to view, naturally disposes of the ashes by the rubbing, and thereby helps to perfect the illusion.

The Falling Matchbox Spirit Knocks Duck Decapitation

● THIS month we present, for the first effect, a method of striking a match on a matchbox falling through the air. The demonstration is as follows: the conjurer removes a match (of the wooden, kitchen variety) from a box, and holds it between his thumb and first finger. He now throws the matchbox into the air, and as it descends, he apparently manages to strike and light the match upon the side of the box. Although this seems to be a feat which can only be accomplished after years of practice, in reality, it is a magical trick which requires but a small piece of apparatus to accomplish.

The "feke" consists of a small brass tube, somewhat shorter than the match. To the lower edge of this tube, a small collar has been soldered, and the inside of the upper end of the tube has been filed rough (if the reader prefers, he may glue a small collar of emery cloth upon the inside of the tube, instead). The "feke," with the match inside, is held between the fingers, as illustrated, and by applying pressure with his thumb upon the end of the match, the match is forced through the tube and automatically lighted. The "feke" is painted in imitation match-color and, at a short distance, is completely invisible.

Perhaps one of the best methods for obtaining "spirit knocks" which has ever come to the attention of the writer, is explained here for the first time. It has been a closely-guarded secret of one of America's foremost mediums, who gained an international reputation almost completely built upon the ability of presenting this one lone manifestation. Spirit knocks, in

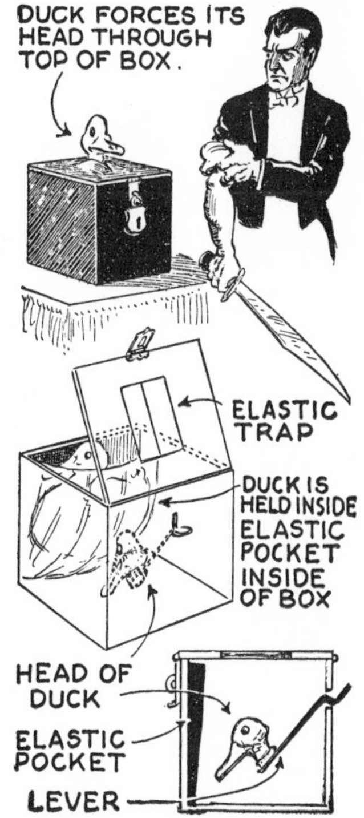

In the duck decapitation, a dummy head is used as illustrated.

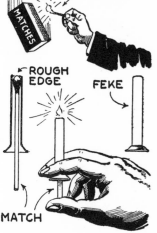

MATCH STRUCK ON FALLING BOX

ROUGH EDGE

FEKE

MATCH

A "feke" which permits one to (apparently) light a match on a falling box.

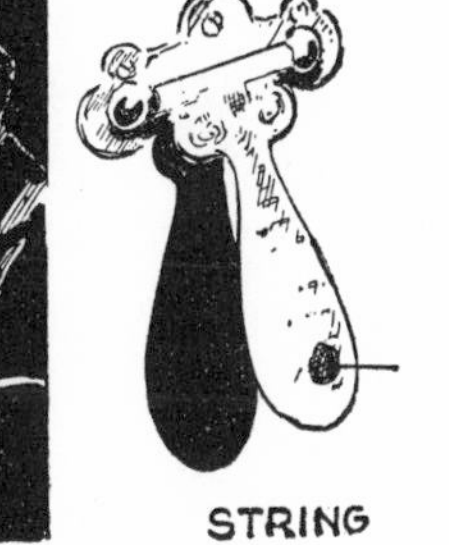

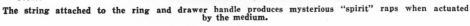

The string attached to the ring and drawer handle produces mysterious "spirit" raps when actuated by the medium.

---

replies to question 5, could be heard about the room, while the medium and a group of believers were seated about the table, with their hands upon the table top, in a manner customary in all spirit rapping seances.

The unusual part of this medium's demonstration consisted in his *power* to produce these raps in almost any strange apartment, and with any table furnished him upon these occasions. The fraud consisted of a fine silk thread tied to his finger ring. To the free end of the thread, a small fiber disc, smeared with beeswax, had been tied. Previous to darkening the room, the medium would secretly stick the beeswax pellet to the handle of a bureau drawer, or the handle of any other similar piece of furniture in the room in which he was demonstrating. When the lights were turned out, he would, by secret manipulation of the thread, pull up the handle and permit it to drop back into place, thereby creating a distinct knock. At the close of the seance, a strong pull upon the thread would free the wax pellet, which, with the thread, was easily disposed of before the lights were turned on again.

For the "duck decapitation" effect, the wizard displays a box, say 14" square. A hinged lid is opened, permitting the spectators to view the interior, and be thereby convinced the box is quite empty. The box is now placed upon a table, and an assistant walks forth, with a live duck beneath his arm, and a huge carving knife in his hand. The duck is thrust into the box, the lid is closed, and the duck is seen to force his head through a trap in the center of the lid. This trap is composed, as the diagram shows, of two strips of elastic webbing, the edges of which have been nailed to the box. Seizing the knife, the magician proceeds to decapitate the duck. Things, however, are far "duckier" than they seem; because the magician pushes the cut-off head back through the trap, and upon opening the box, out hops the duck, as good as ever . . . . flaps his wings, jumps from the table, and utters a few quacks to celebrate his resurrection.

A false head, the neck of which is held in a suitable receptacle, is attached to a lever concealed inside the box. This is the head which is forced through the trap to meet the edge of the knife in the act of decapitation. The duck, of course, is never injured. The head, when replaced in the box, is concealed in the pocket, bordered with rubber-elastic band. This pocket will not show, when the box is shown "empty" at the conclusion of the trick, as the entire interior is painted black.

Chameleon Card New Buried Alive Trick Spirit Candle-Lighting

● HERE is an absolutely new and sensational card effect. The magician places an unopened pack of cards upon the table, and requests a spectator to mention any card in the pack. The spectator is allowed free choice of selection and, let us say, the card he chooses is the nine of hearts. The magician bares his arms to the elbow, and places the enclosed pack of cards upon a small tray, which has been handed to him by an assistant. Tray in hand, he advances toward a group of spectators, selected to act as a committee, in order to prove that the experiment is completely free from deception (the operation involved is performed at close range). Picking up the case, he removes the cards from it, and spreads them fanwise. The backs of the cards are uppermost, save for the one lone card, which had been freely chosen—the nine of hearts. This lone card is reversed, its face standing out in contrast to the backs of the rest of the deck. The card is removed and, upon examination, it is found to be a red-backed card—the balance of the pack being blue backs.

Explanation: A small tray, prepared with a slide or metal pocket, of sufficient size to hold the playing card concealed, is off stage in the hands of an assistant, who also has a complete red-back deck of cards in his possession. When he hears the choice of the card made, he quickly locates the card in the red deck and, after secreting it inside the tray, brings the tray to the magician to place the blue back deck upon. In the act of removing the pack from the tray, the wizard secretly slides the concealed card out of its pocket in the tray, behind the pack; which he proceeds to remove from the case. In nonchalant manner, he gives the cards a single cut, and then spreads them fanwise; which move brings the nine of hearts into the center of the deck.

THE CARD CALLED IS FOUND RIGHT SIDE UP IN CENTER OF NEW DECK.
ASSISTANT BRINGS NEW DECK OF CARDS ON PREPARED TRAY
THE CARD CALLED IS HIDDEN IN TRAY
MAGICIAN PULLS CARD OUT OF POCKET IN TRAY WITH THE NEW DECK.
CARDS ALL BLUE BACKS
THE NINE OF HEARTS HAS RED BACK

The mechanical tray permits any card called for to find its way, apparently, into the middle of the deck, where it appears face up; its back is of a different color.

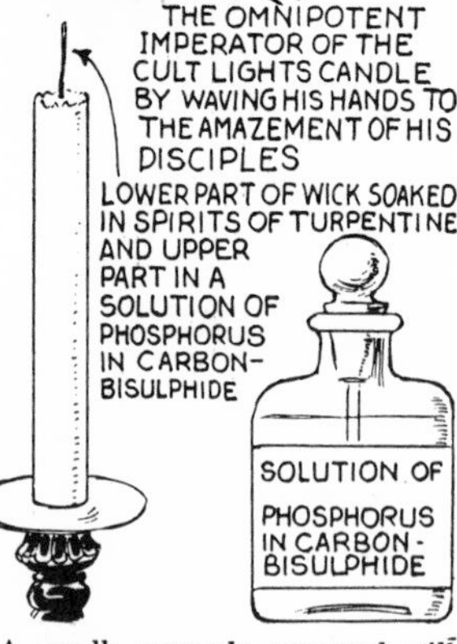
THE OMNIPOTENT IMPERATOR OF THE CULT LIGHTS CANDLE BY WAVING HIS HANDS TO THE AMAZEMENT OF HIS DISCIPLES
LOWER PART OF WICK SOAKED IN SPIRITS OF TURPENTINE AND UPPER PART IN A SOLUTION OF PHOSPHORUS IN CARBON-BISULPHIDE
SOLUTION OF PHOSPHORUS IN CARBON-BISULPHIDE

A candle properly prepared will burst into flame, a few minutes later.

YOGI LIES MOTIONLESS WITH HEAD COVERED WITH SAND IN A STATE OF SUSPENDED ANIMATION ?
METAL HOOD
PIPE IN MOUTH
SAND
SHRUBBERY COVERS AIR INTAKE
PIPE UNDER GROUND

Seemingly in a cataleptic state, the Hindu mystic lies quite motionless, his head being covered with a pile of sand. Thanks to a metal hood and an underground pipe line, he gets all the air necessary for sustaining life.

A European psychic's universal reputation was gained by presenting this "Spirit Candle-Lighting" effect before various groups of gullible cult members. The explanation of this minor phenomenon is as simple as the trick is effective. The medium would assume what he termed a "state of spiritual impulse" and, after the singing of hymns, and the chanting of prayers, his black-robed attendant would bring forth a tray, supporting a candle in a candlestick; which he would rest upon an unprepared table in the center of the room. The group of spectators would sit in a circle, holding hands around the candle, and the medium, at some distance, would make fantastic passes with his hands, in its direction. In a few moments, the candle's wick would burst into flame, and the candle would continue to burn freely; while the spectators would be requested to examine it, to prove it free from preparation, and to convince them that it was mysteriously ignited only through the mystic power of the operator.

Explanation: directly before carrying the candle into the room, the medium's assistant would see that the lower part of the wick (which should be rather long) was well soaked with spirits of turpentine, and the upper part soaked with a solution of phosphorus dissolved in carbon bisulphide. The chemical action causes it to burst into flame within a minute or more. The entire presentation is naturally timed to permit the medium to stage his so-called "spirit" abracadabra.

The next effect is reported to be India's new version of their historically-famous "Buried Alive" mystery. A human form, is seen lying upon his back, with a huge heap of sand piled upon his head. He lies quite motionless and, when a few coins are passed to his attendant, the latter explains that the man is in a state of suspended animation and, to prove that he requires no air whatever, the sand pile has been shoveled over his head.

The charlatan however, does not explain that a metal helmet beneath the pile prevents the sand from coming into actual contact with the face of the wonder-worker. A tube, with one end in the wizard's mouth, has been buried below the ground; while the free end comes up into the air, behind some shrubbery, eight or ten yards away from the fakir's body. Although our performer is not comfortable, he is at least being supplied with sufficient oxygen to keep him alive indefinitely.

"Inexhaustible Box" for Magicians

● BROADLY speaking, we may divide the art of Magic into two classes—sleights of hand, and illusions.

The deft performer of the first-mentioned class has acquired his skill after spending endless hours in patient practice of various manipulations with billiard balls, cards, thimbles, and other small articles, which are, generally speaking, readily obtainable. His success chiefly lies in deceiving his audience by the quickness of his hands, combined with his skill at misdirection.

The performer of the latter class relies almost solely on the smooth working of his cunningly-designed apparatus, also accompanied (of course) by good showmanship. His tricks are essentially of a more spectacular nature, and consequently have entailed a considerable financial outlay.

The drawings on this page represent the "Inexhaustible Box," and in good hands it gives a wonderful effect. In presenting the trick, the box is first shown closed, and turned round exposing all sides, apparently proving that there can be no trickery from the outside.

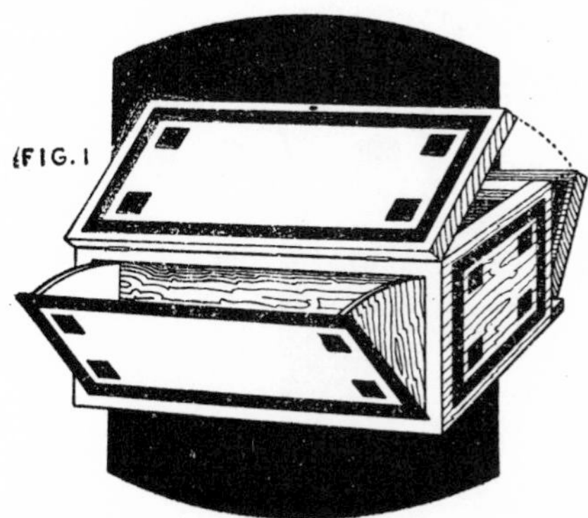

When the inside of the box is examined from the front, the flap compartment swings to the back as here shown.

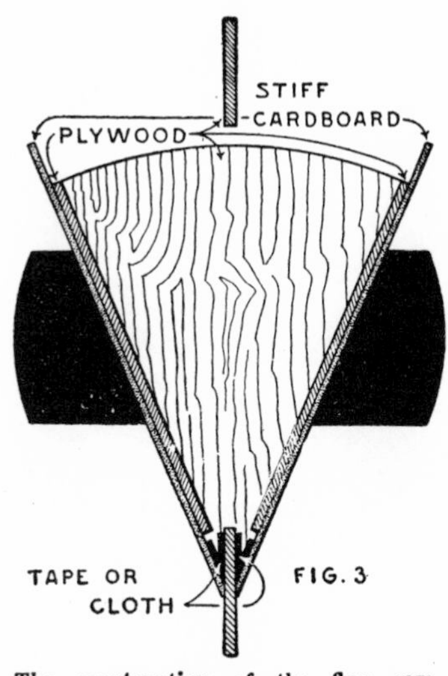

The construction of the flap compartment is given in the above diagram. Note how it stops on either side.

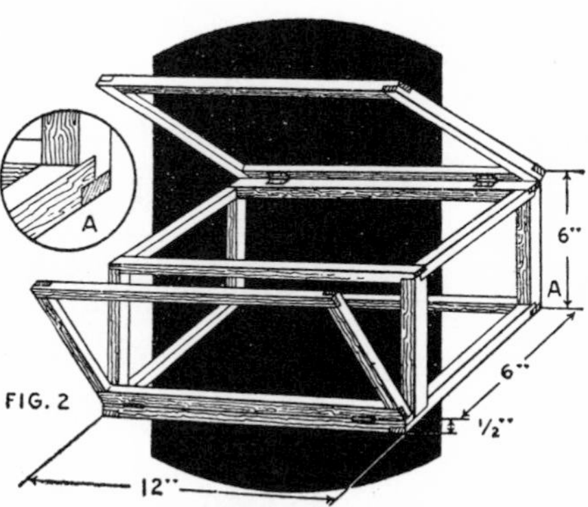

Dimensions of the magician's inexhaustible box are given in this diagram. Insert at A shows detail of a corner.

It is then turned face to the audience, and the two doors are opened, showing the inside to be perfectly empty; the hand or a wand may be passed inside, proving the absence of mirrors. The two doors are then closed, and the box may again be turned round, to face the audience, and the top door opened—when a quantity of colored silk handkerchiefs, ribbons, lanterns, and many other articles capable of compression (so beloved by magicians), are withdrawn; their bulk being apparently beyond the capacity of the box. They should be well spread out, as they emerge, to increase the illusion of bulk; and the result is a most wonderful effect. The box may be again shown inside and out at the finish of the trick, taking care not to expose the secret.

A glance at Fig. 1 will give a general idea of how the box is worked. The back, although apparently the same as the other sides, contains a movable compartment which is swivelled at the bottom. The "load" is, before the showing, placed in this receptacle; the weight allowing it to remain in position either inside or outside the box, at a light push by the performer. Its presence is effectively concealed, when closed, by the border design; which is the same on all sides, thus materially helping the illusion.

The best articles for production are silk handkerchiefs, ribbons, lanterns, small decorated cups that fit into each other, and many other collapsible novelties, all of which may be obtained from a dealer in magic.

These should be folded into as small a space as possible, well down in the secret compartment so as not to impede its movement. The silk handkerchiefs, ribbons, and flags should be carefully rolled up and placed in first, as these have a tendency to expand prematurely.

With regard to the construction of the box, three-ply wood is used for the panelling and doors. This is fixed to a framework of wood ½" square, which is halved and glued at the corners as shown in Fig. 2. For the doors, two small pairs of brass hinges are used. A catch should be fixed on the door front (though not necessary for the top door) to hold it closed.

Fig. 3 explains the construction of the movable compartment; it should form an angle of about 45 degrees. The compartment is first made of three-ply wood, but kept slightly clear of the bottom of the opening, as shown. Fairly stiff cardboard is then glued on each face; allow it to overlap about ½" on the sides and top to conceal the joint, and act as a stop.

The completed compartment is finally made to tip by gluing the bottom of each side to the panel with strong tape or cloth, as shown in the diagram.

It will be found easier to fix the two sheets of cardboard to the panel first and then, when dry, glue in the plywood.

Regarding the decorating of the box, the border design must, of course, be the same both inside and outside of the box; but, if a fancy design is added within the borders, according to the ability of the performer, it will improve greatly the general appearance. Any bright colors may be used, except green which, for a stage show, is not popular.

Handkerchiefs can be made, apparently, to change color by previous placing substitutes inside the secret compartment.

As the concluding trick to your show, you can cause red, white, and blue handkerchiefs to disappear (into the compartment (and a silk flag, of considerable size, to appear in their place.

Music from the Spiritland
Changing Card Trick
Enchanted Demon

THE first trick this month is a clever impromptu experiment requiring no special apparatus and but little practice. In effect, it is one of the most mystifying tricks that one could possibly find. Some years ago, it was offered by an eminent European spiritualist, who even demonstrated it to scientific groups without its secret being detected. An ordinary tumbler is passed for inspection, after which a loop of thread is tied near the top of the glass; the free end of the thread is tied around a round pencil, the loop being loose enough to slip, but not freely. In brilliant light, or what is commonly known as a daylight seance, the medium sits in the center of the room holding the pencil at its end; the glass is visible to all. Soon a mysterious "ting" is distinctly heard; it emanates from the tumbler. After several of these clear, bell-like sounds are heard, the medium advises that the spirits are present, and the glass will answer questions for the believers . . . one "ting" for no, two for yes.

An extremely novel and mysterious trick in which the glass gives forth sounds in "response" to questions. No secret devices are used.

Strange as it may seem, this "music from the spirit land" is created by nothing more than the slightest twist of the pencil held in the outstretched hand. This twist cannot be seen by the most careful observer. By analysis, one will discover that the thread slips suddenly on the pencil, and the vibrations, communicated to the glass,

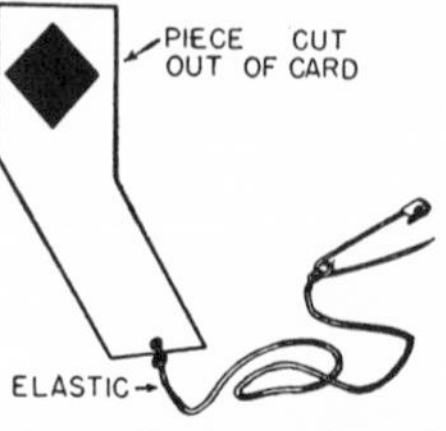

A small piece of card, cut out as illustrated, is affixed to a rubber band running up the sleeve.

The trey of diamonds is converted into the deuce in a flash.

cause it to give forth a characteristic note. The closer the ear is held to the glass, the louder the sound, and the greater the mystery.

Many and varied are the experiments in which an instantaneous change of a playing card is required. There are many forms of changing cards upon the market, but these are all mechanical, and, for that reason, cannot be passed for inspection. Here is a changing card, the suite of which is instantly transformed and the card is then passed for examination immediately. We will say a card has been selected, (forced), and, after it has been reshuffled into the pack, the deck is handed to the magician, who, glancing through the deck, removes a card which he hopes will be the one secretly selected. Holding aloft the trey of diamonds in full view, the magician is informed that the two of diamonds was the one selected and, as is common, the audience expresses the usual amusement at the wizard's failure. Yet, when the magician asks them to take another look at the card, the merriment is reversed, because what seemed to be a trey of diamonds is distinctly found to be the deuce of diamonds.

This effective transformation is accomplished by a small piece of apparatus in the form of an extra piece of a playing card, cut to the shape illustrated and affixed to a rubber band running up the performer's sleeve, where it is attached to a safety pin. Thus, at the proper time, the small piece of card is carried up the sleeve and out of sight. By holding this at a short distance from the spectators, the effect is startling.

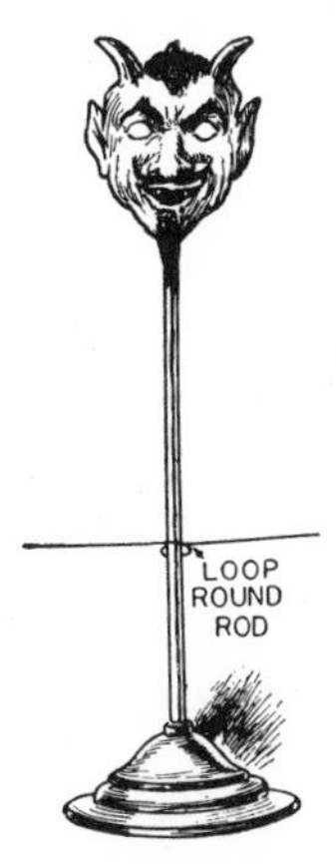

A thread looped around the upright stick makes this head twist or turn.

An excellent effect, suitable for either drawing room or stage, is this small Enchanted Demon. The apparatus is of simple construction and lends itself to a very effective illusion. One first secures a small "doll" face, preferably resembling a demon, such as is sold by novelty shops for masquerading or Halloweʼen celebrations. A dowel about two feet long is attached to the face and is set into a hole in a heavy metal base (commonly used for window display purposes, and securable at any window display supply house). At the wizard's command, the head turns either to the right or to the left or spins slowly or rapidly, in either direction. All of the apparatus may be passed for inspection, and no solution to the mystery can be found. The magician's old pal, the silk thread, is again called upon to assist. A loop wound around the stand, as illustrated, is quite invisible at a short distance. When the stick is placed into the hole of the stand, the thread is secretly moved up into position, which enables operation of the head by two assistants in the wings who simply pull the thread in either direction.

The head is manipulated by two assistants off-stage. It can be passed for examination whenever any member of the audience expresses a desire to do so.

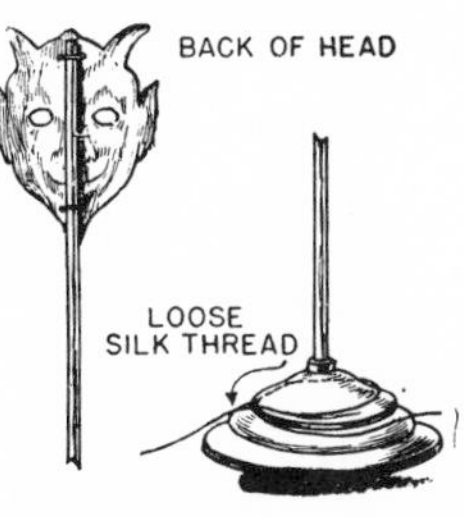

Prior to the experiment the thread is looped around the base. The magician lifts it into position on the dowel when ready to demonstrate.

No-practice Ventriloquism
The Book Miracle
The Enchanted Tie

RADIO and stage ventriloquism is at its peak today. However, ventriloquism can achieve a glamorous value only after many years of persistent practice. Yet, the average amateur, devoting much time to ventriloquial development, soon learns that try as he will, he cannot control lip movements to the degree necessary for perfecting the illusion of the dummy maintaining the conversation.

A piece of apparatus can be constructed easily by anyone handy with tools; it not alone negates the years of necessary practice but assures the operator of perfection. A phonograph mechanism is concealed under the top of a table which stands upon the platform as a prop. Resting upon this table is a glass of water, a pack of cigarettes, matches, etc. A phonograph record of the dummy's dialogue, recorded previous to the performance, is set in action on the concealed phonograph. A wire lever, projecting from the apparatus through an opening in the table top, either stops or starts the motor.* The action becomes possible when reaching for a glass, cigarette, or by simply resting the hand nonchalantly upon the table top during the performance. The operator will find that to smoke a cigarette, drink a glass of water, or stuff a handkerchief into his mouth "while talking" is now a simple matter, inasmuch as these apparent obstacles could not interfere with the "dummy's" continuous chatter.

WIRE LEVER STARTS OR STOPS CONCEALED PHONOGRAPH UNDER TABLE-TOP

The voice for the ventriloquist's figure is produced by a record operated by a concealed phonograph.

The Book Miracle is an interesting and impressive experiment which leans more to the psychic, than to the usual array of conjuring. A large book on a table is shown to a group of spectators. They are instructed to select one member who will open the book at any of the hundreds of pages, and for a few moments mentally concentrate upon the first sentences

* It is better to permit the turntable to rotate at full speed all the time, and introduce the pauses for the operator's comments on the record; or, use a clutch mechanism for starting and stopping the record so that there will be no delay in bringing the record up to proper operating speed.

on both pages. The spectators also are requested to memorize the numbers of the pages at which the book was opened. Making sure the request was understood, the magician leaves the room; the instructions having been followed, he is recalled. For a few moments the wizard gazes at the eyes of the committee, then apparently concentrates deeply. Suddenly, as though impelled by some strange force, he opens the volume to the exact pages chosen by the spectators and reads to them the sentences they had secretly memorized.

Secret: A human hair is the only apparatus necessary to accomplish this startling experiment. The hair is permanently attached to the cover of the book with a small dab of glue. The hair, which should be about six or seven inches in length, originally lies over the edge of the closed book. The reader will perceive that regardless at which pages the book is opened, the length of hair will drop automatically between the selected pages. Naturally the hair is invisible so far as the spectators are concerned; however, it becomes the secret bookmark which enables the conjurer to perform this miracle.

This is a very simple impromptu trick; the bookmark is a hair glued to the cover of the book. It remains unnoticed by the audience, but it tells the magician the page to which the book was turned.

The Enchanted Tie is a somewhat different magical problem requiring very little practice; it is highly effective in the hands of a skillful operator. A silk tie is passed for examination. The wizard displays a small cloth bag, approximately twelve inches square. After the bag has been turned inside out and reversed to prove it empty, a spectator is requested to tuck the tie into the bag. Holding the bag in one hand at arm's length, the wizard states that a small invisible spirit concealed in the bag, upon command, will manipulate the tie into a fashionable knot. Without further moves, the magician reaches into the bag and pulls forth the tie, mysteriously knotted as predicted.

Secret: Two identical ties are employed; one previously knotted, is concealed in the bag (really a double bag made of three layers of cloth sewed together around three of the sides); this construction naturally forms a double pocket. The magician makes sure that the tie which is passed for examination is placed by the spectator into the empty pocket. At the proper time the wizard need only bring his hand into the other pocket and remove the knotted tie.

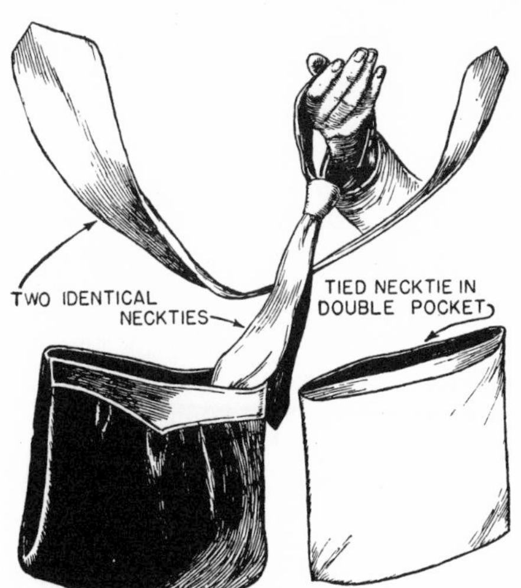

A double bag is responsible for this mystery. A silk tie apparently knots itself within the bag.

Psychic Vision
New Rising Card Effect
Obedient Ball

"Psychic Vision"—in this case the ability to read cards in a pitch-black room—is a simple trick which anyone can do if they know how. The system for producing this effect is described in the accompanying text.

"PSYCHIC VISION" is an excellent so-called mediumistic experiment, which, when properly rehearsed and presented, in effect borders somewhat upon the supernatural. Some of the world's foremost fraudulent mediums have for years demonstrated the trick, and have closely guarded its secret. Because the paraphernalia used is quite ordinary, and the preparation thereof is exceedingly simple, the trick should be extremely effective with the amateur, as well as professional conjurer.

The "medium" is seated in the center of the room, holding an unprepared tray upon his lap. The spectators are requested to write names and addresses upon small blank cards, which are then successively placed, with the writing down, upon the tray. The lights are turned out, leaving the room in total darkness, yet the medium, who has previously gone into an artificial trance, mysteriously reads the contents of the cards, and calls aloud all that has been written thereon, to the acknowledgment of the much amazed spectators.

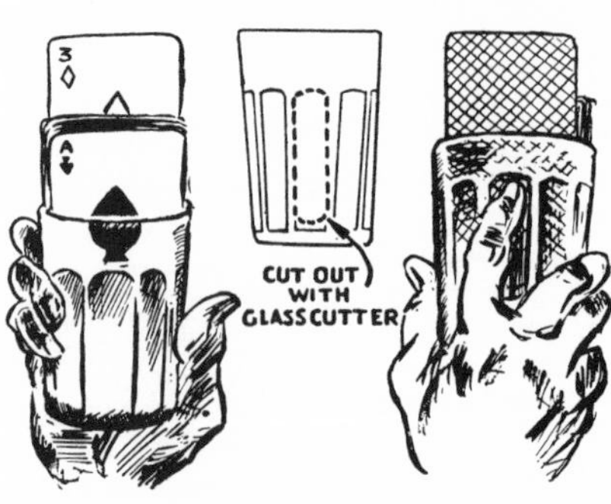

How the selected cards are caused to rise, one at a time, from the glass in which they have been placed.

Right—The method of causing the cards to creep out, by manipulating the index finger through a slot cut in the tumbler.

Explanation: Concealed inside the wizard's pocket wallet (which should be of large size) is glued a fair-sized card, the surface of which is coated with phosphorescent paint. This card had been previously exposed to a strong light for several minutes. The closed wallet is then secreted in the medium's pocket. In the darkened room, he has but to remove the wallet and, by opening the folds, he is able to read the messages upon the various cards, because they are illuminated by the glow of the phosphorescent surface.

A ball is caused to rise and fall mysteriously on the rope upon which it has been threaded. The insert at the left illustrates how the magician's assistant, off-stage, manipulates the movement of the ball.

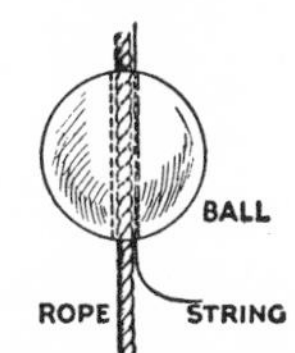

Above — Details showing how ball is threaded on the rope and string at one and the same time.

The next Popular Magic trick we describe is A New Rising Card Effect. Several cards are freely chosen from an unprepared pack and, after their suit has been noted by the persons selecting them, the cards are returned to the deck, which is freely shuffled. The wizard places the deck inside a tumbler, which he holds at arm's length, and requests that the spectators name the cards chosen. As the suits are called, the cards mysteriously rise out of the pack, one by one, rising either slowly or fast, and even returning to the deck, when the spectators request them to do so.

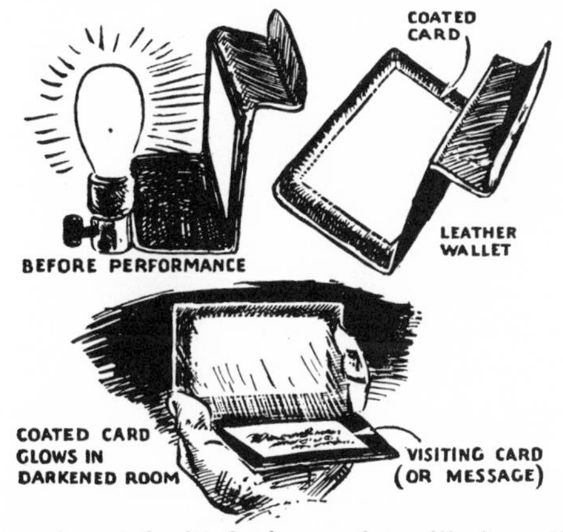

A card, coated with luminous paint, will give sufficient light to read messages in the dark. The wallet screens the light from the observers.

Explanation: The cards are brought to the top of the pack by means of any of the many passes commonly used by amateur or professional magicians alike. If the reader is not familiar with this procedure, it is suggested that he use a deck consisting of two or three suits of cards all alike, and one card of each of the suits is placed on the bottom of the pack beforehand. The top or face card is an odd card, differing from any others in the "forcing" deck. In either event, it is evident that the three chosen cards (or their duplicates) must find their way to the bottom of the pack before it is placed inside the glass tumbler. Unknown to the spectators, a section of the tumbler has been secretly cut away, enabling the magician to cause the cards to rise or descend, by moving his index finger through the open section of the glass. The tumbler should be of a surface design type, as illustrated. The window can be cut in the glass with a glass cutter and then tapping the section out by striking the cut from the inside of the glass. Remove all sharp edges with a wet carborundum stone and polish with fine valve grinding compound.

An "Obedient Ball" is merely a papier mache ball, with a hole drilled clear through. After being passed for examination, a rope is threaded through the ball and the wizard then puts one end of the rope beneath his foot, holding the other in his outstretched hand, as illustrated. At the wizard's command the ball mysteriously rises, and travels upward along the rope, only to descend to the ground again. The spectators are permitted to call aloud the intervals at which they would like the ball to stop during its travels. It stops, travels downward, upward, as dictated by the spectators, and can be made to answer questions by moving once for no and twice for yes.

Explanation: A fine silk thread, of light texture, is again, as in many instances, the invisible friend of the magician. The illustration clearly shows the method with which the ball is threaded and the manner in which it is operated over a concealed pulley, by the magician's assistant concealed in the wings, or behind a curtain.

Rabbit Production Deluxe
Resurrected Card
Colored Rods

MANY years ago the writer originated this effect which he termed "Rabbit Production Deluxe"; he presented it before many well-known magicians who were completely mystified as to the method used. In effect, the audience sees a wooden box frame resting upon a chair seat. The lid is standing against the back of a chair and the bottom of the box is set loosely on the frame. The magician picks up the top in one hand and the four-sided unit in the other and exhibits both freely. The audience can see that neither the bottom nor the sides are fitted with secret compartments. Assembling the box the magician lightly rests the top in its proper position and apparently realizing that the audience has not had an opportunity to examine this top, he removes it instantly and exhibits both sides of the cover to show that this is unprepared. Replacing the cover, he steps back for a few moments and then reaches forward and knocks off the top and a live rabbit comes out of the box. From its interior he then withdraws any of the customary production loads such as silks, ribbons, baby's clothes, etc.

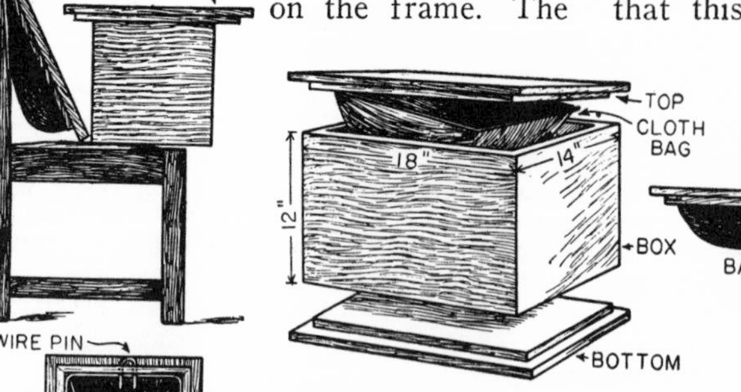

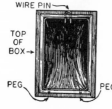

This mystic production box allows for a more careful examination than is possible with similar boxes. It will accommodate a very large load, including a rabbit and, if necessary, several pigeons. The load is contained in the cloth bag affixed to the top of the box, which can be released into the interior by merely withdrawing a pin. The item is set up for stage production, as is illustrated in the diagram at the left.

Explanation: The box itself and the

bottom are entirely unprepared; but, attached to the bottom of the lid is a large cloth bag which holds the rabbit and the production load. This black cloth bag is fastened to a wire frame which fits the top and is held in position by two pins at one end and by a loose-leaf fitting pin, or bolt, at the other end. In its position upon the chair, the audience does not suspect that the load is carried by the lid. Under cover of the misdirections of "testing" the top to demonstrate that it fits, the magician secretly pulls the pin out allowing the entire load to drop into the bottom of the box. So rapid is this movement that the audience never suspects that the load has been transferred. Immediately thereafter, the cover is held up for examination. From this point on the load can be produced at will.

This stage of the divining trick is employed merely to throw the spectators off the track. The manipulations necessary for the successful performance have been accomplished by this time and the magician knows the color of the stick contained within the small metal tube.

ORDINARY ENVELOPE

BACK FROM ENVELOPE—PASTE ROUND EDGE

With the aid of a false back, it becomes possible to resurrect a torn card which makes its appearance on the middle of a ribbon, the ends of which are held by two spectators.

A rather mysterious effect that can be prepared quickly is the resurrected card. In effect, the magician requests a member of the audience to select a card from an unprepared deck. He takes an ordinary envelope and cutting a slit through it, suspends this upon a length of ribbon, the ends of which are held by two spectators. The magician now requests that the spectator tear his selected card into little bits and put them into the suspended envelope, sealing the flap. After a few mysterious passes, the magician tears the envelope open and exposes the selected card suspended from the middle of the ribbon which passes through a slit in the center. Although the results are little short of miraculous,

This is the way the ribbon passes through the envelope. The torn pieces are dropped into the unprepared section of the cover.

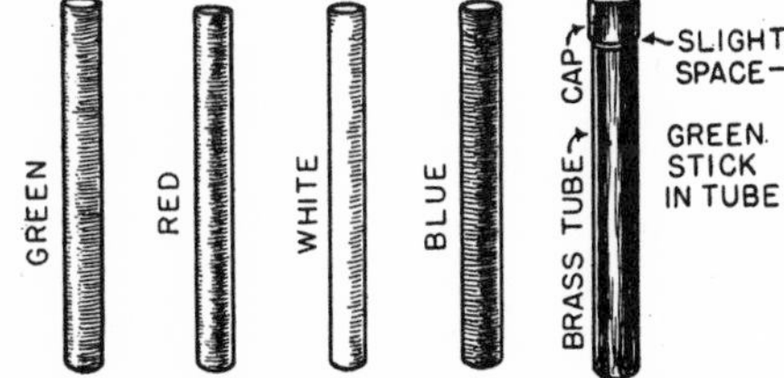

A very slight difference in the thickness and length of these sticks, makes possible an interesting divination effect. All the necessary apparatus can be prepared in one evening.

---

e method of operation is absurdly simple. *Explanation:* Actually, the envelope is uble. There is one ordinary envelope to ıich the back of another envelope had been sted; under this back is a duplicate of the rd to be selected by the spectator. In the t of cutting a slit through the envelope, the agician also cuts a slit through the duplicate rd. Thus, when suspended from the ribbon, e envelope already contains the material necsary for the resurrection. Naturally, the duicate card is forced upon a spectator (or is moved from a forcing deck in which all of e cards are of one suit). When the pieces e torn up and dropped into the suspended velope, they actually fall into the unprered section. Now, when the magician tears en the suspended envelope, he need merely ke care to see to it that none of the torn eces drop to the floor. These, together with the envelope, are crushed between the hands and carelessly tossed aside.

Various divining tricks have originated from time to time; many of them have earned a spot in the programs of present-day magicians. The one here described will be found extremely effective. In demonstration, it is as follows: Four small rods of wood of different colors are passed for inspection, as is a tube into which they fit (many small metal tubes available in pharmaceutical stores could be used for this purpose). During the magician's absence from the room, one of the spectators places a colored wood piece into the tube and conceals the balance. Upon entering the room, the magician holds the metal tube to his forehead and instantly names the color of the wooden dowel which the tube contains.

Explanation: The secret of this trick lies in the fact that although the wooden sticks appear identical, they vary slightly in construction. The green stick is a trifle longer than the rest; the white is a shade thinner and the blue a trifle thicker than either the green or the red. The wizard is able to detect the stick in the metal holder by simple deduction. When the green is inside the metal container the cover does not fit down upon the container tightly. If the white stick is placed into the box, shaking the box up and down announces the presence of this piece by a slight rattle. The red stick does not rattle up and down but will rattle from side to side. The blue one fits perfectly. In making the apparatus, it is merely necessary to cut the sticks all of the same size and increase width or height by the addition of an extra coat of paint.

Second Sight Deluxe
Chinese Coin Release
Hypnotism and the Hot Ball

Although the "medium" is blindfolded she is able to announce the correct value of the cards as rapidly as they are peeled off the face of a shuffled deck. This experiment is very easy to master.

THE first magical effect to be presented this month might be termed "Second Sight Deluxe"—for this demonstration, the "medium" sits upon a chair, facing her audience, and is then blindfolded. The magician, after having explained the weird powers of "second-sight" possessed by the young lady, offers a brand new and unopened pack of cards to a spectator, who is requested to remove the cards from the package and shuffle them, after which other members of the audience are requested to do the same. The magician returns to the stage with the shuffled cards and stands directly in back of the young lady. Holding the deck in outstretched hands, the cards facing the audience, the medium announces the value of every card in order, the wizard

APPARATUS ATTACHED TO BACK OF DRESS

Left—The "servant" which attaches to the back of the medium's dress and permits the magician to exchange the shuffled deck for one containing an orderly arrangement of cards.

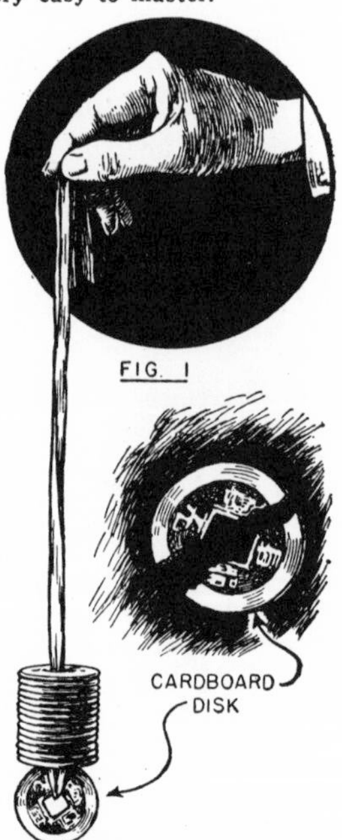

Chinese coins, threaded on a ribbon, are removed under cover of a handkerchief even though the spectator holds the free ends of the ribbon. The cardboard disc is responsible.

removing one card after another as quickly as they are called.

Explanation: Behind the lady's back and attached to her dress is a piece of apparatus consisting of a small bag fastened to a wire frame; this is secured to a flat metal strip fitted with a spring clip which securely holds a duplicate deck of cards. This deck has been carefully "stacked"; the arrangement of the cards is known to the young lady. The magician, upon returning to the platform with the shuffled deck, secretly drops this pack into the bag, meanwhile exchanging it for the prearranged deck. The substitution is easily accomplished in the act of adjusting the lady's blindfold. Properly presented, this is one of the most effective of all "second-sight" tricks. Various forms of arrangement as to suits and numbers of the cards, will suggest themselves to the reader.

A spectator is requested to hold a metal ball and is then informed that it will become so hot he will have to drop it. The "hypnotic" effect surprises the audience.

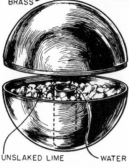

HOLLOW BRASS

UNSLAKED LIME

WATER

This illustration explains why the ball heats up. Water coming in contact with unslaked lime produces enough heat to make it uncomfortable to hold the brass ball. Make sure the ball has an air vent.

Two stages in the demonstration of removing coins from a ribbon. The experiment is performed under cover of a handkerchief.

For the next new effect, a handful of Chinese coins, twelve or fourteen in number, is passed for inspection, together with a piece of ribbon, approximately twenty-four inches long, and about a half inch wide. The articles are returned to the conjurer, who passes the ribbon through the center of one of the coins, and then, holding both free ends of the ribbon together, the balance of the coins are threaded upon the ribbon, as illustrated in Fig. 1. The ribbon and its coins are now presented to a spectator, who is requested to hold the ribbon firmly between his fingers, thereby making it quite impossible for any of the coins to be removed. The wizard now conceals the spectator's hand by covering it with a borrowed handkerchief, and, reaching below the covering, all the coins are mysteriously removed while the ribbon is left intact. All the articles are instantly passed for inspection.

Explanation: All of the coins are genuine Chinese coins, with the exception of one which is an imitation made of cardboard, and decorated to resemble the genuine. The cardboard disc, of course, is retained secretly in the performer's hand, while the genuine coins and ribbon are passed for inspection. The "coin" threaded upon the lower end of the ribbon is the cardboard one. Reaching beneath the kerchief, the magician finds no difficulty in releasing the stack of coins, inasmuch as he has but to tear the bottom cardboard coin to remove it; this releases all the others.

For the last effect to be described this month, the magician greets his audience with a lecture concerning his powers of hypnosis and, in order to prove his ability of mind over mind, he invites the most skeptical member of his audience to the platform. Needless to state, no difficulty is ever experienced in finding a skeptic among a group witnessing a conjurer's demonstration. As the confident individual walks forward, the magician displays a metal ball, which he explains, will clearly help to demonstrate his hypnotic ability. The ball, approximately 2½" in diameter, of polished brass, is placed in the palm of the skeptic's outstretched hand, and the magician requests that he inform the audience whether or not the ball is of the average cool temperature. The audience is assured that the metal is quite cool, and the magician explains that he will hypnotize the subject, making him believe, by hypnotic control, that the ball will become so hot in his hand, that he will be unable to retain it—what is more, it will become so hot no one in the audience could hold it. In spite of the skeptic's broad smile and self-assurance, the magician makes several fantastic passes before his eyes when, after a few moments, with a loud yell, the skeptic drops the ball to the floor, and briskly rubs his hand, which apparently has been burned.

Explanation: The ball is made of two half shells, threaded to enable the magician to screw the two parts together, thereby forming a perfect sphere. A short metal tube is soldered into one of the shells. This contains a small quantity of water. Inside the ball surrounding this tube, the magician has placed several pieces of unslaked lime. In presenting the effect, the magician, after having given the ball to the skeptic, turns it upside down. The water and lime, coming in contact with each other, quickly causes the ball to become so hot that it is impossible for the spectator to hold it. The hypnosis part of the demonstration is but a bit of cleverly arranged showmanship—to introduce what is nothing more than a clever conjurer's trick.

"Off with his head" — and his head comes off.

Decapitation

REMOVING a man's head has for years been symbolic of magic, and although lithographs descriptive of this somewhat gruesome act have graced the covers of many magical publications, no really practical method of performing the trick, of a nature inexpensive to construct, has been described heretofore.

The illusion herein exposed is an extremely effective method, requiring simple apparatus, which anyone the least bit handy with tools, can construct.

The effect consists of a hooded executioner, swinging a heavy blow with an axe, the sharp edge of which strikes the neck of the supposed victim, who is kneeling upon the floor, his head resting upon the edge of an innocent looking block. The head, appar-

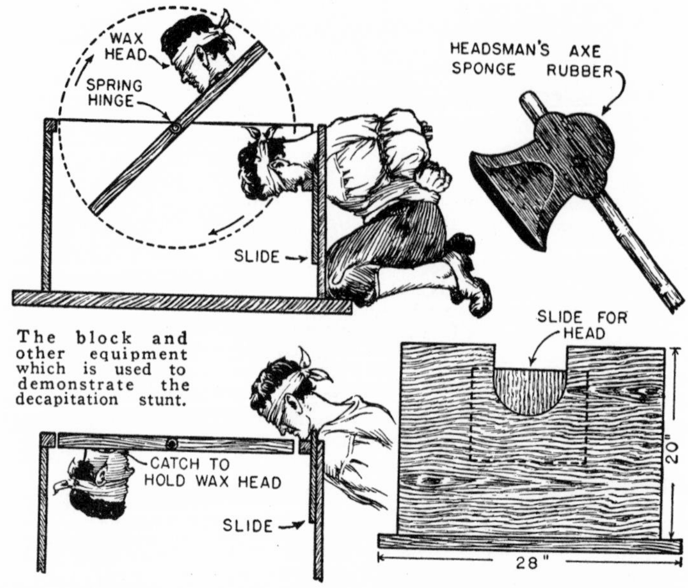

The block and other equipment which is used to demonstrate the decapitation stunt.

ently severed from the body, is lifted into the air by the executioner, the lifeless and headless form remaining in clear view of the audience, as the curtains close upon the scene.

The diagram shows clearly how really comfortable and uninjured the victim is, throughout the entire demonstration. The block is mechanical. A revolving panel in the top spins around, concealing the assistant's head, and carries to view a head of wax, which has been previously concealed inside the block. A slide in the side wall of the block permits the assistant to find a convenient and concealed space in which his head is comfortable, and yet is hidden from the view of the spectators. A section of, or the entire axe, is sponge rubber, lending itself perfectly harmless should it strike the victim's neck as it falls. When properly timed, the assistant can get his head out of the way. A wooden axe could be substituted then.

Magical Dexterity

THE conjurer borrows a half dollar, which is marked for identification. He now passes for inspection an ordinary table knife, which is found unprepared. With steady hand, the edge of the coin is now balanced upon the sharp edge of the knife, and by dexterous manipulation, is made to roll from one end of the knife to the other. Both coin and knife may again be inspected after the experiment.

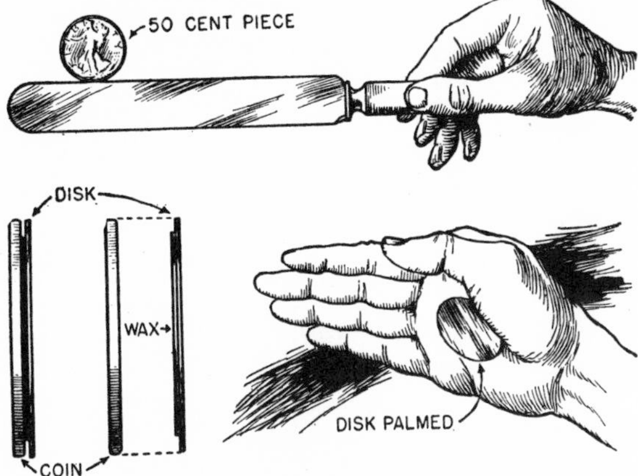

By means of the small féke, palmed by the magician, it is possible for him to balance a coin on edge on the blade of a knife.

Although the trick seems to be one of expert jugglery, requiring years of diligent practise, it is in reality a conjuring trick, quite simple to execute. The trick is dependent upon a small metal féke, in the form of a disk (the size of a half dollar), which the performer has previously palmed, and which secretly clings to the borrowed coin, by means of some beeswax, which has been smeared upon the flat surface of the disk. Thus, the matter of balancing the coin upon the edge of the knife is truly simple, as the groove formed between the disk and coin forms a convenient track. The disk is secretly palmed after the presentation and the half dollar and knife passed for inspection. The disk is made of two pieces of metal, soldered together, one slightly smaller than the other.

An enlargement of a photograph on a card appears mysteriously on the face of a mirror when the magician fires the torn bits of card in the direction of a frame mounted on a table.

The Enchanted Mirror
The Demon Touch
The Darting Ping-Pong Ball

THE *Enchanted Mirror* is an exceptional and startling effect which, although highly mystifying in presentation, requires apparatus which can easily be constructed by the average person within a few hours. Standing upon the table and facing the audience, is a mirror, mounted in a two-inch frame, supported upon a wooden stand. The wizard produces a pack of cards, consisting of fifty-two pictures of various celebrities, such as Presidents of the U. S., rulers of foreign countries, or persons otherwise universally recognized. One of these cards is freely selected by a spectator, and the name of the person whose picture it reproduces is called aloud. The magician tears the card into bits, and stuffs the pieces inside a funnel-shaped attachment affixed to a revolver. Standing some ten odd feet away from the mirror, the magician fires the gun in the direction of the glass, when, much to the amazement of the spectators, a portrait corresponding with the one on the previously selected card, appears mysteriously upon the surface of the mirror.

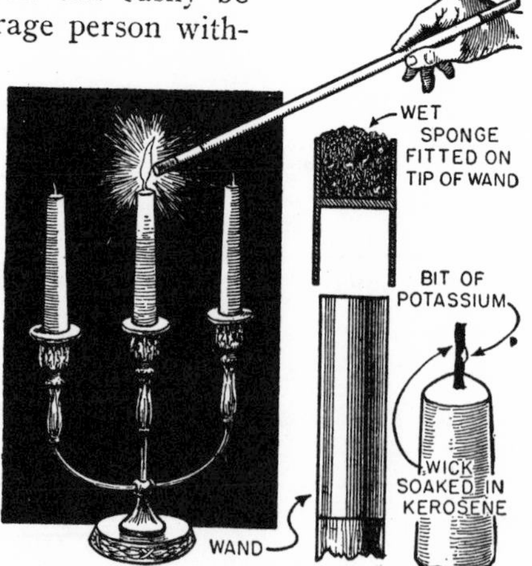

Touching the tips of the candles with a wand they light mysteriously. Candles and wand are then passed for examination. The diagram explains how the trick is done.

Explanation: The mirror really consists of two mirrors, one of which slides up and down freely, inside the wooden frame and conceals from view the picture of the celebrity, which has been secretly painted upon the surface of the glass beneath. As the shot is fired, an assistant "off stage" pulls a string releasing a pin which permits the loose mirror to slide in its groove out of the frame, through a slit in the table top, and into a padded well or bag made to receive it. The playing card, containing the portrait corresponding with the "spirit" picture, is "forced" upon the spectator. The pictures can

A celluloid ball floating on the surface of the water moves around at great rapidity and bobs up and down when the hands are mysteriously passed over the surface. A frightened fish produces the effect.

Below are shown the details of the apparatus for producing the picture on the mirror, illustrated at the top of the previous page.

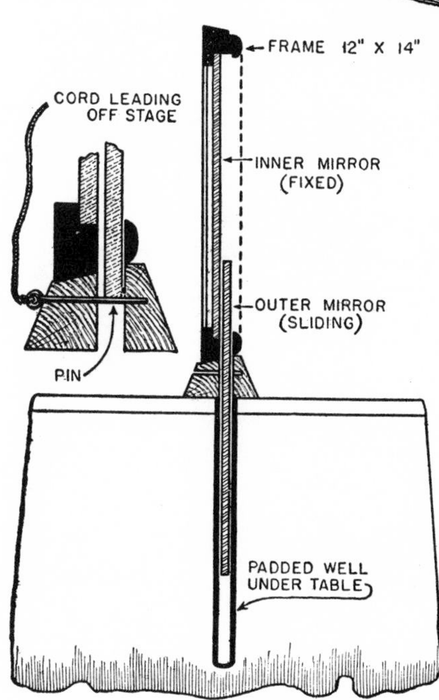

either be drawn upon the cards by hand, or may be cut from magazines or newspapers and pasted upon the cards.

The *Demon Touch* is one of those weird and creepy effects, which generally leave so marked an impression upon the average audience. Resting upon the magician's table stands a candelabrum, each of the arms supporting a candle of usual and ordinary appearance. The wizard takes his magic wand and slowly touches the wick of one of the candles, and it instantly bursts into flame, and continues to burn in natural manner. This phenomenal effect is repeated with the other two candles, which are likewise ignited in the same mysterious fashion. The wizard now carries the candle stick containing the burning candles, together with the wand, to his audience, who, upon inspection, pronounce the candle stick, candles, and wand, entirely free from preparation.

Explanation: The secret, as in most effective illusions, is extremely simple. Each candle is prepared before the presentation, by soaking the wick with kerosene, and secreting, in the fiber of the wick, a small piece of metallic potassium. The wand has a cap which fits over the tip, inside of which rests a small piece of sponge, which has been soaked with water. When the moist sponge comes in contact with the potassium, it instantly bursts into flame and ignites the wick. After production of the effect, the extra wand tip secretly slides off the wand, and is disposed of, enabling the magician to pass all of the apparatus for inspection.

From the streets of Calcutta, in the land of the mystic East, there comes another story which heralds the mystic power of the miracle men of India. Seated beneath the shade of the palm tree can be seen the long bearded picturesque brown man of India, performing an experiment which has not only baffled scientists, but many of the occidental magicians as well. Resting upon the ground is an earthen bowl, which contains some muddy water, and floating upon the surface thereof is a two-inch ball of celluloid, which has been painted with bright oil colors. The wizard has but to extend his serpentine fingers and hold his hand several feet above the bowl, to cause the ball to dart up and down and in various directions upon the surface of the water. Each time he utters his weird chant and extends his magnetic hand, the ball darts about, as if alive, resting only at the intervals in which his hand is withdrawn. After several demonstrations of this weird power have been offered, he grasps the ball, and passes it for inspection among the bewildered spectators.

Explanation: Attached to the celluloid (ping-pong) ball, is a short silk thread, the free end of which is tied to a small fish. The fish is quite invisible beneath the surface of the muddy water. As the wizard waves his hand over the bowl, the fish becomes alarmed, and starts to dart about, carrying the ball with it, and thereby causing it to move. When the ball is removed and passed for inspection, the magician releases it from its pellet of bees-wax, which frees it from the silk thread and the fish, both of which remain concealed below the surface of the water.

Memorized Dictionary Feat
Touch Identification of Cigarettes
Threading the Thumb Trick

The magician is proving, to the satisfaction of the audience, that he has memorized every word in the dictionary and its location.

THE first effect to be described this month requires but little preparation. The magician leaves the platform, carrying with him a large Webster's dictionary, which he passes for inspection, and which is found quite unprepared. He explains to his audience that he has mastered the gigantic feat of having memorized each word in the entire dictionary, and its actual location therein. The wizard returns to the platform, and requests that a committee of several members of the audience (with whom the dictionary has been left), open to any one of its pages, and count down to any one word upon that page. After the word is decided upon by the committee, they call aloud to the wizard, and request that, for example, he answer the question, "What is the one-hundred-and-fourth word, on page 709?" The magician concentrates deeply, then, reaching for a slate and piece of chalk, he writes something upon its surface. He now requests the committee to call aloud the selected word, so as to acquaint the rest of the audience with it; for example, we will say the word was "inexplicable." At the moment the word is called, the magician turns the slate about, and to the amazed audience, the word is found written upon the slate in very bold letters.

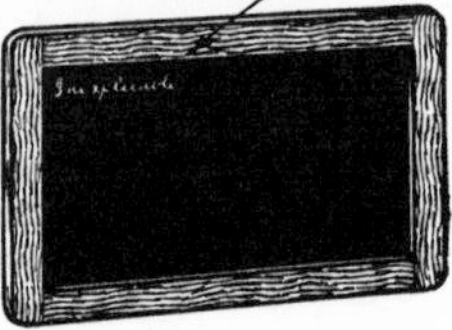

The slate which is handed to the magician is prepared in this fashion by his off-stage assistant.

Explanation: As in most great magical effects, the secret is unusually simple. Unknown to the audience, the conjurer has two dictionaries, exactly alike, one of which is in the hands of an off-stage assistant, standing in the wings. As the page and the number of the word is called aloud by the committee, the assistant quickly finds the page and locates the word in the duplicate dictionary. He writes this in small letters in the upper corner of the slate, and holds it in readiness for the performer, who nonchalantly reaches off stage for the slate. After secretly familiarizing himself with the word, he makes a copy thereof in bold, large

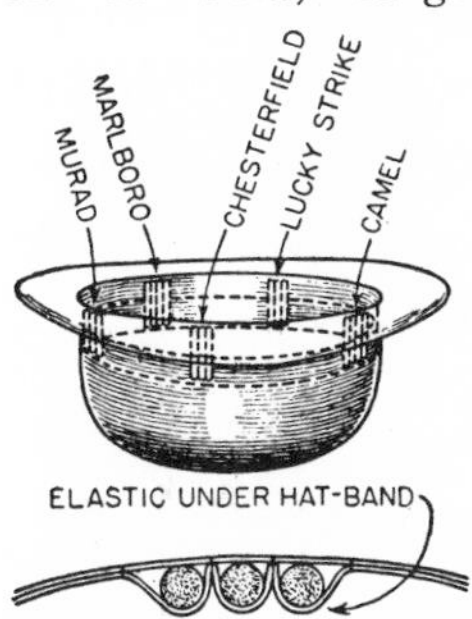

The magician can name any cigarette by touch as he draws it out of the hat and also can produce any popular brand of cigarette when it is called for by the audience. The diagrams explain how it is done.

letters and with his thumb secretly eradicates the small memorandum.

For a long time one manufacturer of a popular cigarette advertised a blindfold test. The strange thing about such a test is that the average person cannot tell one cigarette from any other of the same type. Try it and be convinced. But in this demonstration the magician disdains taste—he names the cigarettes by touch alone!

Several packs of cigarettes of various brands are opened by a committee, and the cigarettes are emptied into a derby hat. The blindfolded magician reaches into the hat, which is held by a volunteer spectator, and pulls forth a cigarette. This, though blindfolded, he designates as a "Camel," and tosses it out into the audience for identification. Again reaching inside the hat, he pulls forth a "Chesterfield," then a "Lucky," now an "Old Gold," etc., all of which are identified to be correct in accordance with the conjurer's calling.

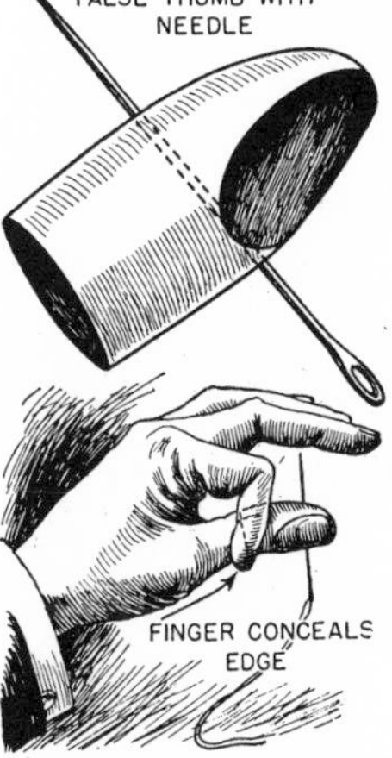

With this equipment the magician is able to demonstrate that he can run a needle and thread through his "thumb" painlessly.

Explanation: Concealed below the hat band several strips of elastic have been sewed to form pockets; each holds a few cigarettes. The wizard need only memorize the groups, in their order, to pull forth a cigarette of a desired brand. To strengthen the effect, the audience may choose their own brand, which they call aloud to the performer and, as he knows where to find such a cigarette, he can produce it immediately. Some fussing in the bottom of the hat will make the trick appear more difficult. Next, the magician patters about the holy men of the East and describes to his audience that many of their self-inflicted tortures are painless to the victims, only because they have the will power to disregard pain. Not to be outdone by this oriental wizardry, the conjurer slowly passes a previously examined darning needle and thread through his thumb. The thread is drawn to and fro through the pierced thumb, apparently without ill effect. Needle and thread are then withdrawn and the magician allows his audience to examine his hand; no one is able to discover the slightest mark of injury.

Explanation: The magician's friend, the false thumb (a flesh-colored piece, fitting over the natural, in thimble fashion) is responsible for this effective deception. A small hole has been drilled through the metal, through which needle and thread actually pass. By holding the hand, with the thumb attached, as illustrated—the forefinger concealing the edge of the artificial thumb—the illusion is perfect. After presenting the trick, the thumb is easily disposed of in the act of placing the needle and thread upon a table. Naturally, nothing now prevents a free and complete examination of the performer's hand.

Balancing Glass
Diabolical Smoke
Spirit Messages

BALANCING a glass of water on a piece of rope stretched across two chairs is a new and startling effect, suitable for either drawing room, or stage presentation and, although the trick is extremely simple to perform, it has an uncanny effect upon the audience. An examined rope and glass tumbler are passed for inspection. Upon return of the articles the rope is tied to the arms of two chairs, separated a short distance (approximately six feet apart). The magician half fills the glass with water, pouring the liquid out of a pitcher. His arms bared to the elbows, the conjurer sets out to balance the glass upon the edge of the rope at a point about half way between the two chairs, as illustrated. Slowly he releases the glass, leaving it mysteriously suspended in this impossible position, apparently under the spell of his outstretched fingers, much to the amazement of the onlookers.

Explanation: Before presenting the trick, the wizard secretly tied a length of thin strong silk thread between the two chairs. At a short distance, the thread is entirely invisible. It is this thread which holds the glass in position. Little experimentation will teach the performer exactly how to place the glass, to balance the same properly.

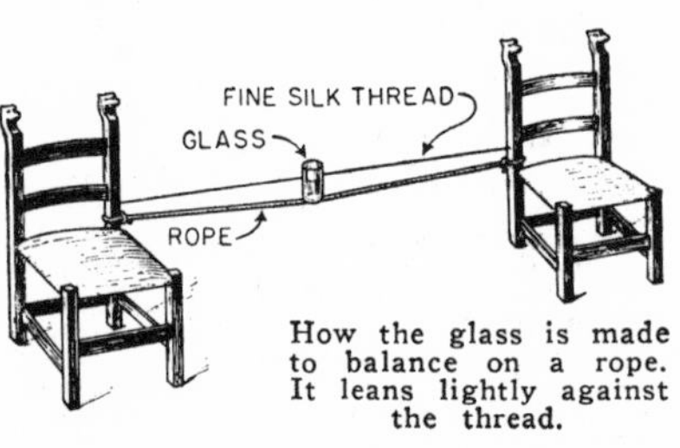

How the glass is made to balance on a rope. It leans lightly against the thread.

"Diabolical Smoke" is an extremely effective combination trick, with a highly professional touch, requiring little preparation, and comparatively little skill to perform. The magician borrows a handkerchief from a member of his audience; upon receiving same, he places it upon the table, then he exhibits a transparent goblet, and a plate. Placing the goblet upon the table, the wizard crowds the handkerchief inside the glass, and covers the top of the goblet with the inverted plate. Prior to this procedure, a card selected by another member of his audience has been retained by that person, who is now asked to call aloud the suit of his selection. We will assume it to be the trey of diamonds. Lifting the plate from the goblet, large clouds of smoke puff forth. Upon removing the kerchief, an exact replica of the trey of diamonds, in color, is found imprinted mysteriously upon the borrowed handkerchief.

Explanation: The card is forced; for the amateur not sufficiently skilled, it is advisable that a deck of all cards of one suit be used. Therefore, as the entertainer is familiar with the value of the chosen card, he has prepared a wooden block of the trey of diamonds, which has been inked with red rubber stamp ink, and then embedded, face up, in the table top. As the borrowed handkerchief is momentarily stretched over the table, a secret impression of the card is obtained. The clouds of smoke are produced by wetting the surface of the plate with a few drops of hydrochloric acid, and placing a few drops of strong ammonia inside the goblet. The reaction of the two chemicals produces the smoke.

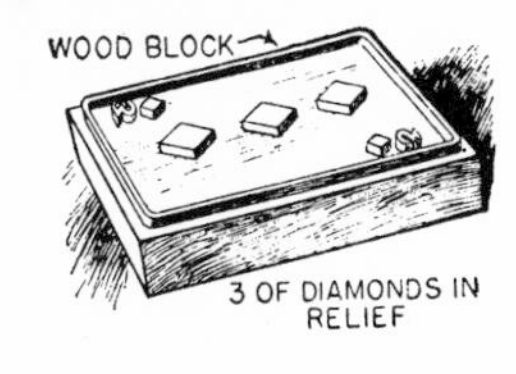

The wood block which applies the impression of a card to the handkerchief.

Displaying the impression of the selected card on the handkerchief.

Above—How the table is set up for the card mystery. This also shows how the print on the card is obtained.

Left — The false thumb (greatly exaggerated) holds the bit of chalk with which the message is written when the slate is held at arm's length.

"Spirit Messages" is the third presentation this month. The magician explains the weakness of mediumistic slate writing, outlining that the phenomenon usually produced in a dark room, is far less effective than demonstrations of a conjurer, who, through skillful trickery and dexterity, is able to produce a message upon a slate in a room, or upon a platform, brilliantly illuminated. The slate in this instance, may be brought by any spectator, in order to prove it is unprepared; or, if desired, any one of a heap of eight or ten unprepared slates, which are freely passed for inspection, may be selected for the experiment. The magician holds the slate at arm's length, as illustrated, yet, although the surfaces of the slate are entirely clean and free from marks when examined, the wizard produces a so-called spirit message. This message may consist of any name freely called by one of the spectators, a person's initials, or the name of a card (if the conjurer wishes to use the slate idea in combination with a card trick).

Explanation: The magician's friend, the false thumb, again acts as his hidden assistant. The thumb is an artificial flesh-colored metal article, which slides over the conjurer's thumb. In this instance, a collar, which tightly grips a small piece of chalk, is soldered to the metal thumb. Holding the slate away from his body, as illustrated, with all of his fingers in view, the audience does not suspect that the message is being written with the thumb, naturally concealed behind the slate.

Spirit Clock
Spinning Doll
Reappearing Card

THE first effect to be described this month is a new "Spirit Clock." A glass disc, 15″ in diameter, with the numerals from 1 to 12 painted upon it, is displayed. Upon examination, the spectators find that the apparatus is entirely free from deception. The only mechanism about the glass disc is a square peg 3″ long, which revolves freely through a bearing in the center of the disc. The magician also passes for inspection a brass pointer, 12″ long, which he places upon the peg, and then suspends the clock freely in mid-air, by means of two hooks tied to two ribbons. Standing some distance away from the apparatus, the magician makes several mysterious passes; the pointer of the clock begins to revolve mysteriously. The spindle moves fast or slow, at the performer's command. Numbers may be called by the audience, and the pointer always stops at the chosen number. Selected cards may likewise be registered, by having the spindle stop at a number corresponding with the number of spots on the card selected.

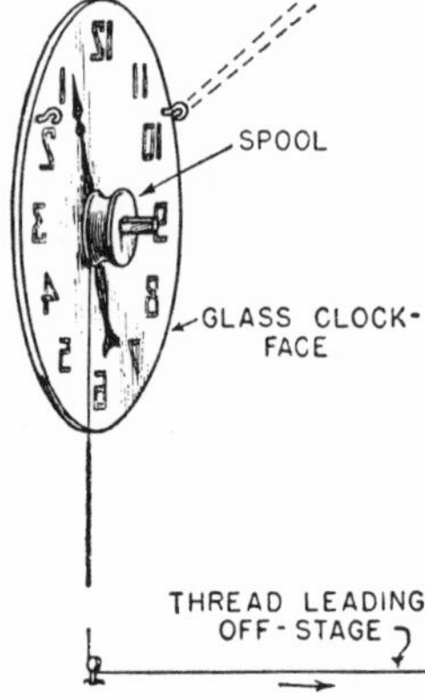

Explanation: Unknown to the spectator, the conjurer has secretly plugged a small spool of silk thread in back of the projecting peg. The free end of this thread is in the hands of an offstage assistant, who begins to unwind the spool, and as the thread is pulled, the pointer revolves. The assistant behind the wings takes such a position that he can get a full view of the clock; therefore he is able to stop at any

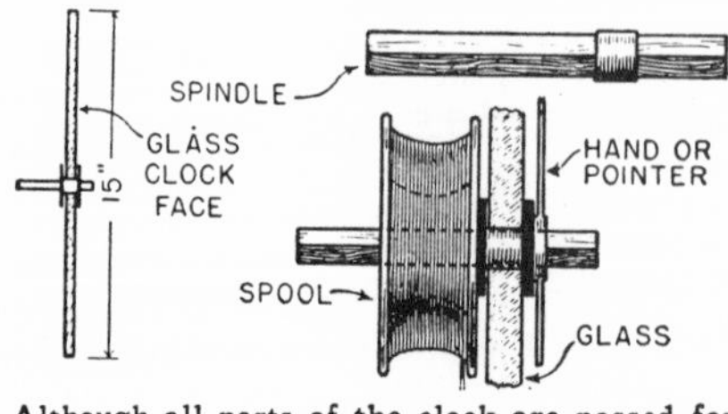

Although all parts of the clock are passed for examination, the working feature, that is, the spool is secretly attached while the magician is hanging the clock face from the ribbons. By this means the clock can be made to stop at any predetermined position.

desired number. When registering the number of a chosen playing card, the assistant knows its value because the card is "forced." The simplicity in construction of the apparatus should make this a very desirable addition to any program for both amateur or professional magician.

A very simple apparatus can be constructed quickly for causing a card to appear attached to the cork of a bottle. As will be observed, the card is concealed in a pocket formed by the label.

India, the oriental home of mystery, again supplies us with a native experiment. It is one of the most mystifying of oriental tricks and perhaps one of the least known secrets in this country. The conjurer, turban clad, and with his legs folded beneath him, sits upon the ground while his assistant passes a length

You can amuse yourself with this simple parlor stunt. Soak a straw in water and, when thoroughly wet, twist it and set aside to dry. When the straw becomes moist it will unwind and can be made to produce a startling effect.

of straw for inspection. A small figure of a doll, cut from a peacock's feather, is also examined, and found unprepared. When the items are returned to the conjurer, he carefully ties the doll to the tip of the straw with a small piece of thread. He now sticks the straw into the ground, for a distance of 2″, and moving some feet away from the apparatus, he begins to play a weird tune upon his flagolet, while his assistant calls upon the mystic spirits. Mysteriously and slowly, the doll begins to spin about, and for some minutes this weird phenomenon continues, much to the amazement of the onlookers.

Like most oriental mysteries, the secret of this startling effect is exceedingly simple. Several days prior to the demonstration the magician soaked the straw in a basin of water. When quite soft, the straw is twisted dozens of times, after which it is placed in the sun to dry. The straw is planted into soil which has been previously moistened and, after several minutes, the moisture is absorbed, and the straw begins to untwist, which action causes the feather doll to spin.

Although highly mystifying this third experiment calls for apparatus which can be constructed in a short space of time. The effect—the magician has a card chosen from the pack, and after the value and suit have been noted by the spectator, the card is torn into bits; the pieces are loaded into a funnel-shaped tube affixed to the muzzle of the magician's pistol. Standing some distance away from a corked quart bottle, the magician fires in its direction. The card, completely restored, instantly appears attached to the cork.

Explanation: A duplicate card is necessary. It is originally concealed inside a pocket, cleverly made from a wine-bottle label, the upper end of which is open, allowing the card to be drawn out of the pocket and into position upon the cork. A fine black silk thread, secretly attached to the card and passing through the hole in the cork carries it up. The free end of the string is in the hands of an off-stage assistant. A flat weight, glued near the edge of the card, properly balances it so that it remains upright and sand in the bottle prevents tipping.

Chinese Lantern and Scarves Trick
Disappearing Kerchief
Jumping Coin Trick

ORIENTAL tricks are most desirable with present-day audiences, lending themselves, as they do, to much color and mystery. The effect about to be described is doubly desirable, as it is simple to construct and comparatively easy to operate. A large Chinese lantern of the folded paper variety is freely shown to be unprepared and is placed, in folded fashion, upon the magician's table, after which the arms are bared to the elbows. Again taking the lantern and opening it to its fullest extent, the wizard reaches inside and pulls forth dozens of kerchiefs of various colors, flags, ribbons, silks, paper flowers and other spectacular production materials, which every magician uses.

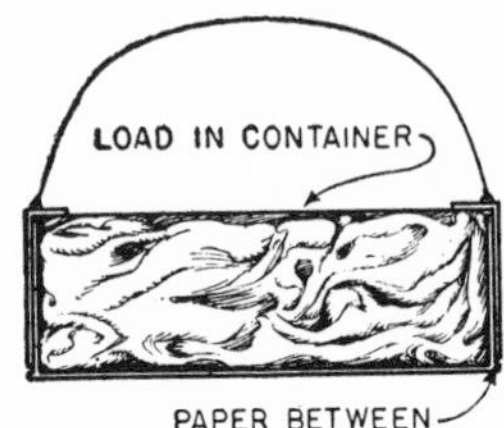

A container just large enough to slide into the bottom of a Japanese lantern holds the material which later will be "produced" from within the folded paper construction. This container fits into a recess in the top of the table. When the lantern is lifted the container is secretly conveyed up into it.

Explanation: The silks previously were tightly loaded within a metal container—a round tin box over the top of which a sheet of paper had been forced and held in place by a metal ring slightly larger than the box itself. This feke, thus prepared, was carefully hidden inside a well in the magician's table, where it remained hidden from view, save for a projecting wire loop, painted black and invisible at a very short distance. The folded lantern having been placed over the loaded feke in the table, is carried from the table together with the load. Of course, the reader understands that the bottom of the lantern had been removed to permit the feke to enter.

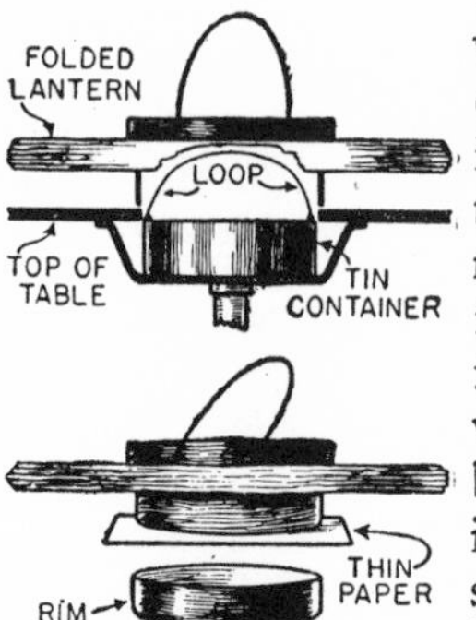

The second effect, presented here, is an extremely effective and ingenious method of vanishing a handkerchief, and which, when presented with a little practice, will puzzle even an expert.

The magician folds a silk handkerchief into the smallest possible dimensions. To prevent it unfolding, he encircles it with an ordinary red rubber band taken from his pocket. Baring his arms to the elbow, he holds the package between his hands, when, like a flash, it disappears. Bringing his hands together again, it reappears quite as mysteriously. The explanation lies in the fact that through the rubber ring a length of flesh - colored silk thread has been passed; the ends of the thread are tied together. In the act of setting the handkerchief comfortably under the rubber band, the wizard secretly passes his forefinger through the loop thus formed. A slight upward movement flips the little package to the back of the hand, where it remains completely concealed. Reversing this move causes it to reappear. With a bit of practice the conjurer is able to show both back and front of the hands "all clear" several times before the reappearance of the kerchief; of course, the handkerchief each time is transferred to the side of the hand remote from the audience.

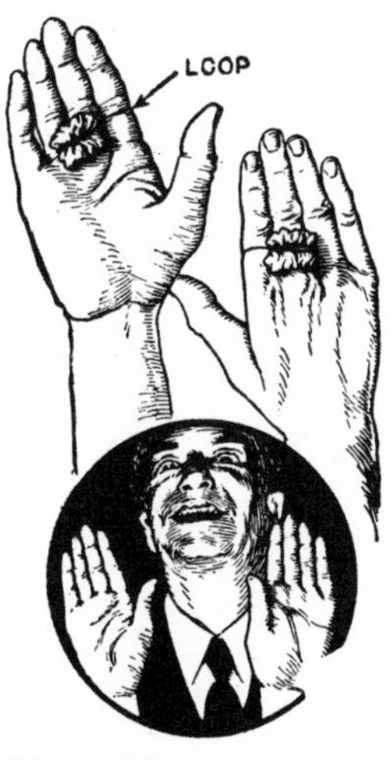

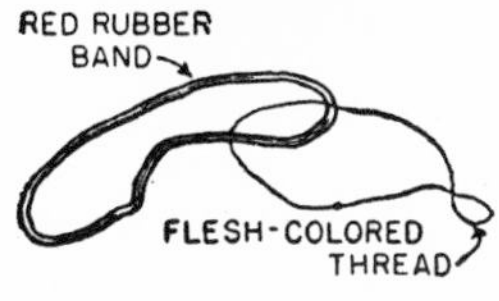

A rubber band and a loop of flesh-colored thread is responsible for the silk handkerchief vanish. Actually the handkerchief is flipped from the front to the back of the hand, and vice versa.

It is an accepted fact that the realm of conjuring involves every known branch of mechanics, electricity and chemistry, yet the latter is perhaps the least employed, as there are but few chemicals found practical for obtaining magical effects. Contrary, however, to this generally accepted rule, is the effect here described. A borrowed coin is handed to a spectator, and he is told that by rubbing it and repeating some magical word, the coin will mysteriously jump out of his hand. The result is as was predicted; the friction sets up a harmless explosion, which not only causes the coin to jump, but likewise disturbs any nervous spectator.

A chemical on a coin explodes when lightly rubbed, much to the surprise of the voluntary assistant and the spectators.

Explanation: The borrowed coin was exchanged secretly for a duplicate coin, which had been prepared previously with a little dab of iodine fulminate, made as here described: Reduce a very few flakes of ordinary iodine to powder, place into a small glass, and add a teaspoonful of liquid ammonia. After the mixture stands for about one-half hour, it is filtered through paper, leaving behind a *dark* brown substance, the chemical formula of which is NH_3I_2. While still wet, it should be divided into minute portions, each about as large as a grape seed; each portion is put on fresh blotting paper to rid it of superfluous moisture and, while still damp, one of these small portions is transferred to the coin. When dry, the lightest friction will cause it to explode. It is well to remember that all such chemicals are dangerous in careless hands and should be handled only in accordance with instructions. Do not mix in large portions and keep no stock.

Drum of Mystery
Cigarette Magic
Match Box Monté

Obtaining a large quantity of silks from an "empty" drum.

THE "Drum of Mystery" is a trick suitable for either drawing room or stage. The magician displays a metal cylinder, open at both ends, and holds it up so that the audience may look clear through, thereby proving the same to be empty and unprepared. The cylinder is then placed upon an undraped table, and the wizard converts it into a drum by placing ordinary sheets of newspaper upon the top and bottom thereof, holding the paper in position by forcing a hoop, or rim, over each end. The drum is then suspended upon a skeleton stand. Piercing the paper in the center of the drum with his finger, the wonder worker reaches inside, and pulls forth yards of vari-colored ribbons, rainbow-tinted kerchiefs, silk foulards, flags of various nations, etc.

Explanation: As the diagram discloses, the drum has an inner section (cone shaped) which is soldered firmly to the edge of the cylinder. The space thus provided is packed with the ribbons and silks before the presentation of the trick. The audience, permitted to look through the cylinder, is unable to discover the inner lining (such a construction cannot be detected at even a very short distance).

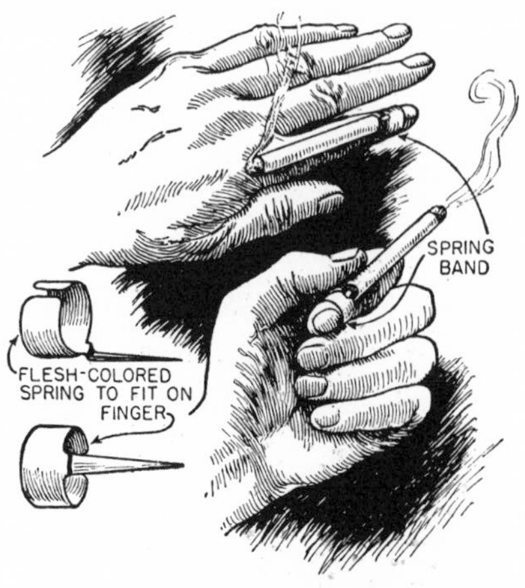

This simple instrument will enable the user to vanish, or produce a lighted cigarette at will. Keep the hand moving in air so that the smoke will not be visible.

Note. This presentation and method of performing this ever popular trick is far in advance of the one used by professional magicians for a number of years, which requires a specially constructed table for loading the drum.

Cigarette magic, or the handling of lighted smokes, has always been exceptionally impressive with the average audience. Spectators realize the difficulty in manipulating a lighted cigarette, and therefore credit the entertainer with great ability, if he is able to deceive them by either vanishing, or producing a burning cigarette at will. The apparatus described and illustrated here, consists of a flesh colored metal band, to which is attached a bayonet point about an inch long. The band, which is worn upon the index finger, enables the magician to display freely the palm of his hand, the fingers wide apart, and yet serves to conceal a cigarette in back of the hand. Thus, as illustrated, a lighted cigarette may be either produced or vanished at will. Various passes and unique sleights will suggest themselves to the operator, enabling him to perform effects unusual and mystifying.

In our third experiment this month, three match boxes are displayed on a table. The wizard opens each, proving that two are empty, and the third one contains a dozen or more matches. The boxes are closed and arranged in a row upon the table. The wizard now mixes the boxes up, and at intervals picks up a box, which he shakes, permitting the spectators to hear the rattle of the matches within; then, after mixing the boxes up a bit more, he defies his audience to locate the one containing the matches. Many will try, but they are usually unsuccessful. In reality, the procedure is a form of match box monté, similar to the well-known three card monté.

Explanation: The conjurer has the advantage over his unsuspecting victims, who do not know that, concealed beneath his coat sleeve and tied firmly to his arm with a piece of tape he has an extra match box, containing some loose matches. Therefore, after shifting the matchboxes on the table, he has but to shake one of the empty boxes; the spectators hearing the sound of the matches coming from the concealed box, follow the movements of the empty box when replaced upon the table, and are thus misled as to the actual position of the match-containing matchbox.

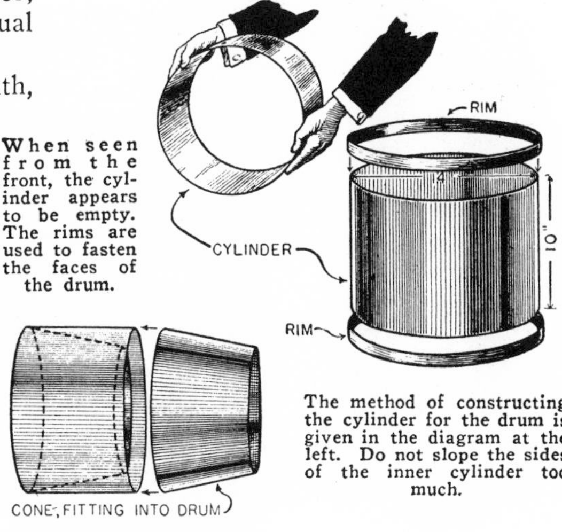

When seen from the front, the cylinder appears to be empty. The rims are used to fasten the faces of the drum.

The method of constructing the cylinder for the drum is given in the diagram at the left. Do not slope the sides of the inner cylinder too much.

DRUM
AUDIENCE LOOKS THROUGH HERE
FLAGS, &C.
NEWSPAPERS, STRETCHED OVER ENDS OF DRUM

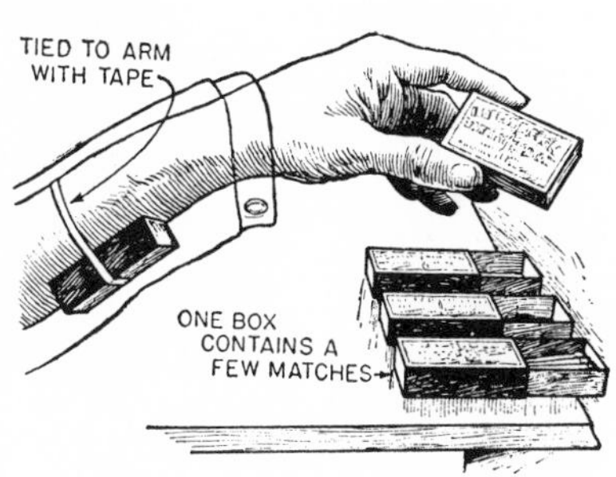

The matchbox, strapped to the wrist, fools the audience into believing that even the empty boxes contain matches. An empty box is lifted, shaken, and it apparently makes a sound, as if it contained matches.

The Spiritualist's Box
Mesmerized Handkerchief
A Mechanical Sleight of Hand

IT has often been said that a poor magician makes a good spirit medium, which is more or less true, in view of the fact that beneath the guise of religious ceremony, the fraudulent medium need not be possessed of any great amount of dexterous training, in order to deceive his subjects. Those who have become ardent believers fall prey easily to any form of deception, be it ever so crude as their anxiety to believe renders them almost helpless to detect fraud, which would otherwise be extremely obvious. Thus, of late, a prominent Russian spiritualist has created a furore by offering a miracle somewhat new in the realm of the supernatural. During the medium's absence from the room, the sitters place various objects into a metal box, which is then locked with a padlock, after which the keyhole is sealed. The medium re-enters the room, and the box with its contents is placed upon her lap. The lights are then turned out and the shades drawn, leaving the room in total darkness. After the usual abracadabra,

After various articles are deposited in a metal box, the box is locked and the keyhole is sealed. With a simple pick the medium can open the lock and, by touch, can determine the contents and then describe the articles in the box.

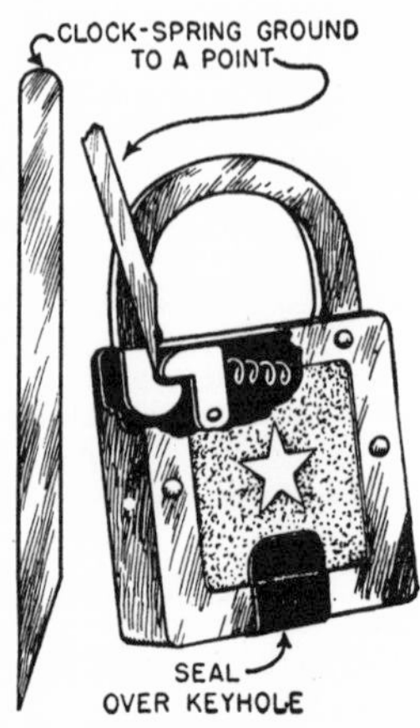

singing of hymns, etc., the medium suddenly interrupts the proceedings, claiming that her "spirit guides" are beside her, and are now prepared to demonstrate spiritualistic powers by describing in detail the various objects concealed in the box. This is actually accomplished, much to the amazement of those attending the seance. After the seance is ended, the box, lock and seal are examined, and everything found quite intact.

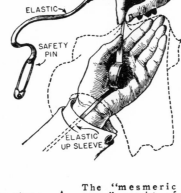

The writer, however, noted that although six or seven locks of varied manufacture were offered for inspection, and one was chosen freely, all the padlocks operated, as the illustration shows, by a single tongue, which snapped under the hook of the arm of the lock. This type of lock is commonly referred to as a snap spring padlock, and is obtainable in any hardware store. A piece of clock spring, filed down to a sharp edge, if inserted as illustrated, enables any operator to push the tongue backward, releasing the arm of the lock. It is a simple matter, therefore, for the "psychic" to open the lock in the darkened room, without interfering or disturbing the seals previously placed over the keyhole. By a sense of touch, the medium can easily feel and describe the various articles inside the box. All material is then replaced and the lock is snapped closed, before the lights are again turned on and the box is offered for inspection.

Effects of a creepy nature are always desirable. The present-day conjurer, both amateur and professional alike, seems to favor tricks attributable to some strange power, rather than to the dexterity of the wizard. This effect is one that leaves a marked impression with an audience, and yet is simple to operate. The wizard requests the loan of a handkerchief, which he opens, and places upon his outstretched palm. With the fingers of his other hand, he grasps the

A handkerchief will assume a standing position on the palm of the hand, when "mesmerized."

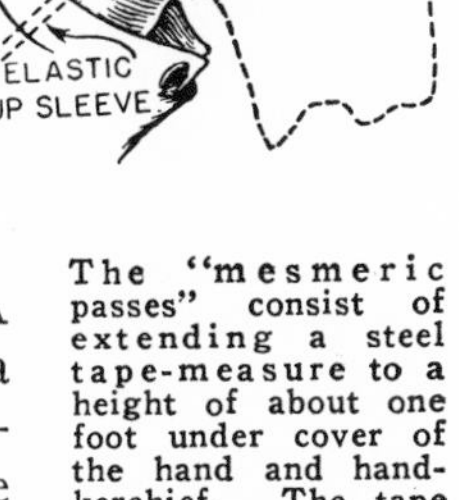

The "mesmeric passes" consist of extending a steel tape-measure to a height of about one foot under cover of the hand and handkerchief. The tape is later vanished up the sleeve.

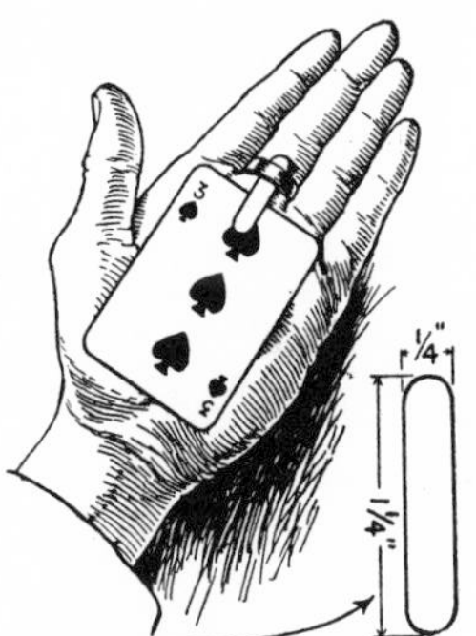

A small piece of flesh-colored steel spring, inserted under the finger ring, will aid in palming various articles.

PIECE OF FLESH-COLORED CLOCK-SPRING

center of the kerchief, and slowly raises it some 12 or 14 inches, and then releases his grasp, when, much to the bewilderment of his spectators, the handkerchief remains suspended in that position. After the miracle has been studied by the group, he again pushes the handkerchief down to its original position, and instantly passes it for inspection. His hands are likewise examined, without a clue to the mystery being discovered.

Explanation: Hardware stores throughout the country are selling a metal tape measure, the case of which is the size of a small pillbox. The tape, when pulled out of the case to a length of 12 or 14 inches, stands rigid and erect. Concealed beneath the kerchief, the magician secretly holds one of these tape measures, which enables him to pull the metal tape up to the desired length, under cover of the handkerchief, thereby causing the illusion. A length of strong elastic, attached to this apparatus, causes it to fly up his sleeve, and out of sight, at the conclusion of the experiment.

Tricks requiring sleight of hand are numerous. The amateur sometimes is obliged to eliminate startling effects from his program, not having fingers trained for this purpose. Palming cards, coins, rings, thimbles, etc., are more or less essential to the average magical routine. The idea here described is a method whereby the amateur can, with very little practice, accomplish feats heretofore entirely beyond his realm. A small piece of clock spring, 1¼" long, and ¼" wide, should be painted flesh color, and then slid beneath the edge of a finger ring. Coins, cards, etc., can then be palmed with ease, by simply sliding the extending edge of the spring over the object, as illustrated. Various additional uses for this simple, yet important piece of apparatus, will suggest themselves to the reader.

Spiritland Messages
Mystifying Cigarette Holder

THE first effect to be described this month is of the spiritualistic type. The "victims" are requested to write questions, and sign their names on small cards, which were distributed by the "medium" before the seance. The cards are collected in a basket, with the writing turned down, and the basket is placed upon the medium's lap. A metal trumpet of the type common in spiritualistic circles, is set on the floor alongside the medium, who, amid the singing of hymns, soon passes into an apparent trance. The lights are now turned out, leaving the room in darkness. After a short time has elapsed, various voices are heard (depending upon the medium's ventriloquial ability and power of mimicry). The voices soon call the sitters by name and, as they identify themselves, the questions upon the cards are mysteriously read and answered, apparently to some degree of satisfaction. The remarkable feature of this demonstration rests in the fact that the medium is able to read messages and names in the dark. Inasmuch as such a feat is generally accepted as impossible, the members of the circle are willing to believe that a supernatural agency is at work.

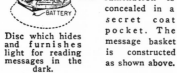

Disc which hides and furnishes light for reading messages in the dark.

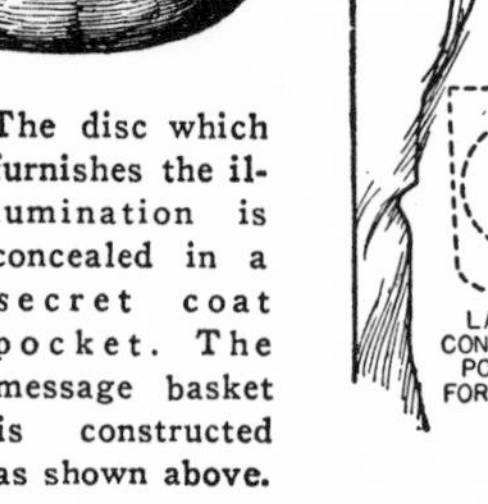

The disc which furnishes the illumination is concealed in a secret coat pocket. The message basket is constructed as shown above.

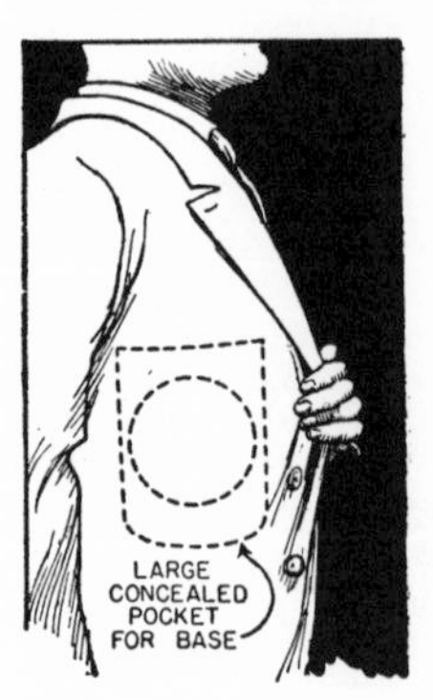

Let's put some light on the subject — for light it truly is, when one realizes that the medium has concealed about his person a piece of appratus which simplifies matters greatly—consisting of a cone-shaped disc fitting the mouth of the trumpet, and completely covering its opening. A flashlight bulb is affixed to the surface of the disc;

the lamp is operated by a button and battery concealed inside the disc. The medium places one card after another beneath a small clip on the surface of the disc and, after adjusting the trumpet and looking down into it, he reads the writing on the cards, now illuminated by the incandescent bulb. Because all of the light is completely concealed in this enclosure, the sitters never suspect the apparatus. The messages naturally are delivered through the trumpet by the medium, and while answers to one message are given, the second message is made ready.

Cigarette tricks are ever popular and the one here explained is simple to perform, and highly mystifying. The magician displays a cigarette, supported in a holder. The cigarette is burning freely and the wizard puffs away in nonchalant manner. He displays his palms, which are unmistakably empty and without preparation. Bringing one of his hands up toward the cigarette, he encircles his fingers around it and removes the cigarette from the holder. He now slowly opens his fingers, to prove that the burning cigarette has been vanished; this mysteriously reappears in the holder. The experiment is repeated as often as may be desired.

The cigarette is apparently covered and removed from the holder by the closing hand. However, this is later shown empty.

A mechanical cigarette holder which makes it possible to vanish a cigarette at will, or cause it to reappear again.

Explanation: The cigarette holder is of mechanical construction. Inside the holder is a small sliding cup, at the end of which the tip of the cigarette is firmly held. By strongly "inhaling," a suction is produced which draws both cup and cigarette inside the holder. Naturally, by blowing through the holder, the cigarette reappears. The reader will, of course, instantly grasp that the cigarette never leaves its holder; the wizard only pretends to hold it in his hand.

Spirit Writing
Cigarette Sleight
The Card Miracle

IN our current issue we offer a baffling trinity of unique and mystifying effects, proper presentation of which will puzzle any audience. Even the craftiest magicians and prestidigitators in the country have scratched their heads over these.

"Spirit" writing always has the approval of the audience. One of the simplest ways of accomplishing such a phenomenon is by the use of a slate, the construction of which is described here.

The magician secures the desired message by any of the various methods well-known to the art. The answer is written upon slate either during the performance, or even while the trick is being demonstrated. (In the latter event, a small piece of chalk is attached to a false finger and is used for the purpose. A description of this apparatus appeared in a previous issue of this magazine.)

Assuming that the magician has established the answer and the slate has been prepared, the effect is as follows: Both sides of the slate are wiped clean with a wet sponge to assure the spectators that the slate has not been chemically prearranged. Both sides of the slate are shown and one side is marked for identification. The slate is then rested upon a table or chair and at word of command the mysterious message appears.

The mechanical slate, illustrated here, makes it possible to produce a "spirit" message instantly. At a short distance the flap cannot be seen by the spectators.

As will be observed in the accompanying diagrams, the slate has a flap of cardboard hinged at the center; for this purpose a cloth hinge may be employed. Cardboard, slate and cloth are painted with imitation slate-paint, procurable at hardware stores. From a short distance the flap cannot be detected. Naturally, it is the back of this slate that is marked for identification. Thus, when the flap is permitted to drop down from its original position, it discloses the message previously written upon its surface. Magicians will appreciate the superiority of this method because it eliminates cumbersome mechanical devices or the cus-

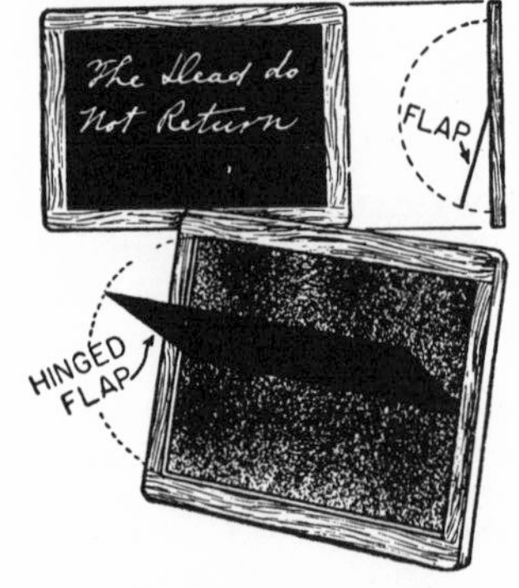

tomary loose flaps. For the card manipulator this slate can be employed in conjunction with any "forcing" procedure.

The second of our magical phenomena is a cigarette sleight. Not limited to club or stage performances, it is used to mystify impromptu groups at close range. With his sleeves bared to the elbows, and without the use of cumbersome knickknacks, the magician is able to spirit away a lighted cigarette and to reproduce it at will. Preparing for this feat requires only a few minutes—the apparatus consists of a small cap of cork colored metal made to fit over the cork tip of a cigarette; and the short end of a needle which is permanently soldered to the cap. The cork color of the metal cap and the position of the cigarette between thumb and forefinger conceal the needle, thus eliminating danger of detection. Before presenting the trick, the magician secures the cap over the cigarette, then stepping confidently before the audience, lights it. Cigarette in hand, he makes a series of up and down movements, pretending to throw the cigarette in midair, while actually pinning it to the sides of his trousers. A few hocus pocus gestures, and he slowly separates his fingers showing the cigarette has vanished. Repeating these movements, possession of the "smoke" is regained. The intervals between disappearance and reappearance must be brief, so that the slow-burning cigarette can do no injury to the clothing.

CIGARETTE PINNED TO CLOTHING

This extremely simple fitting for any "cork tipped" cigarette will permit the amateur magician to vanish a cigarette at will. The needle hooks the cigarette to the clothing, as shown at the left.

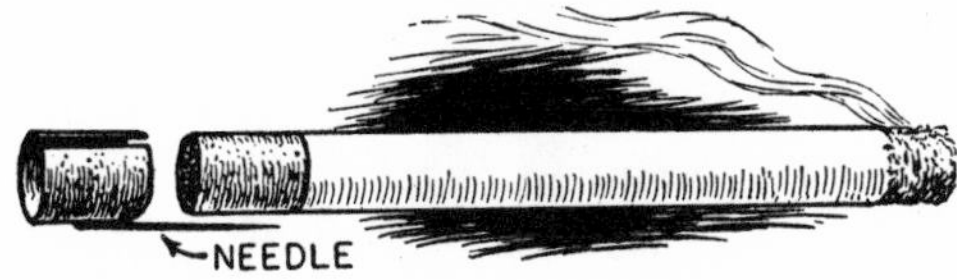

Our third bit of magic, "The Card Miracle," is most dramatic when presented as a psychic experiment. A spectator is invited to examine and shuffle the deck of cards which is then returned to the entertainer. Holding the pack face down in the palm of his hand, the performer slowly removes the top card which is kept facing the audience in such a position that it is thoroughly impossible for the magician to see the suit. Pressing the card to his forehead he feigns a psychic impression and calls the suit correctly. Fifteen to twenty cards he holds to his head in like fashion, and names each precisely. Then he gathers up the cards, passes the pack for reshuffling and immediately duplicates his success.

The trick formula for the foregoing is simple: all the cards are unprepared except one, to the corner of which has been glued a small triangle of glass mirror (or a highly polished triangle of chrome-plated metal). While the pack is being shuffled by a spectator, this key card is secretly retained in the magician's palm and upon return of the deck is unobtrusively placed at the bottom. If the mirror end of the key card is allowed to protrude slightly from the pack, as illustrated, the pip or index of each card removed from the pack will be reflected in it. Should the experiment be repeated, the prepared card is palmed, of course, while the pack is passed for the second shuffling.

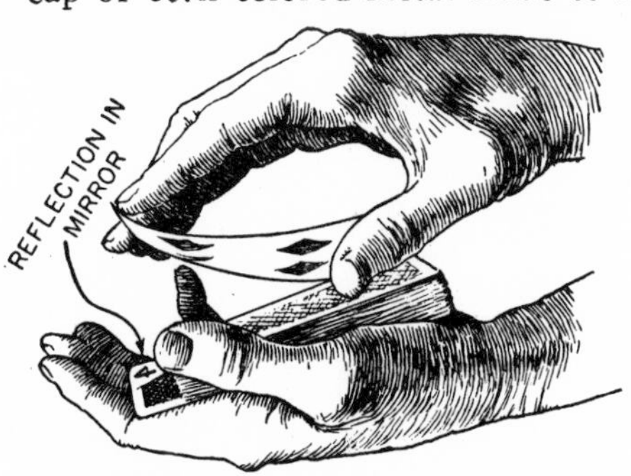

An interesting method of permitting the magician to determine the value of any card is to use the specially prepared bottom card to which a triangular piece of mirror has been fastened.

How the mirror card is prepared.

Historically Famous Mysteries Explained

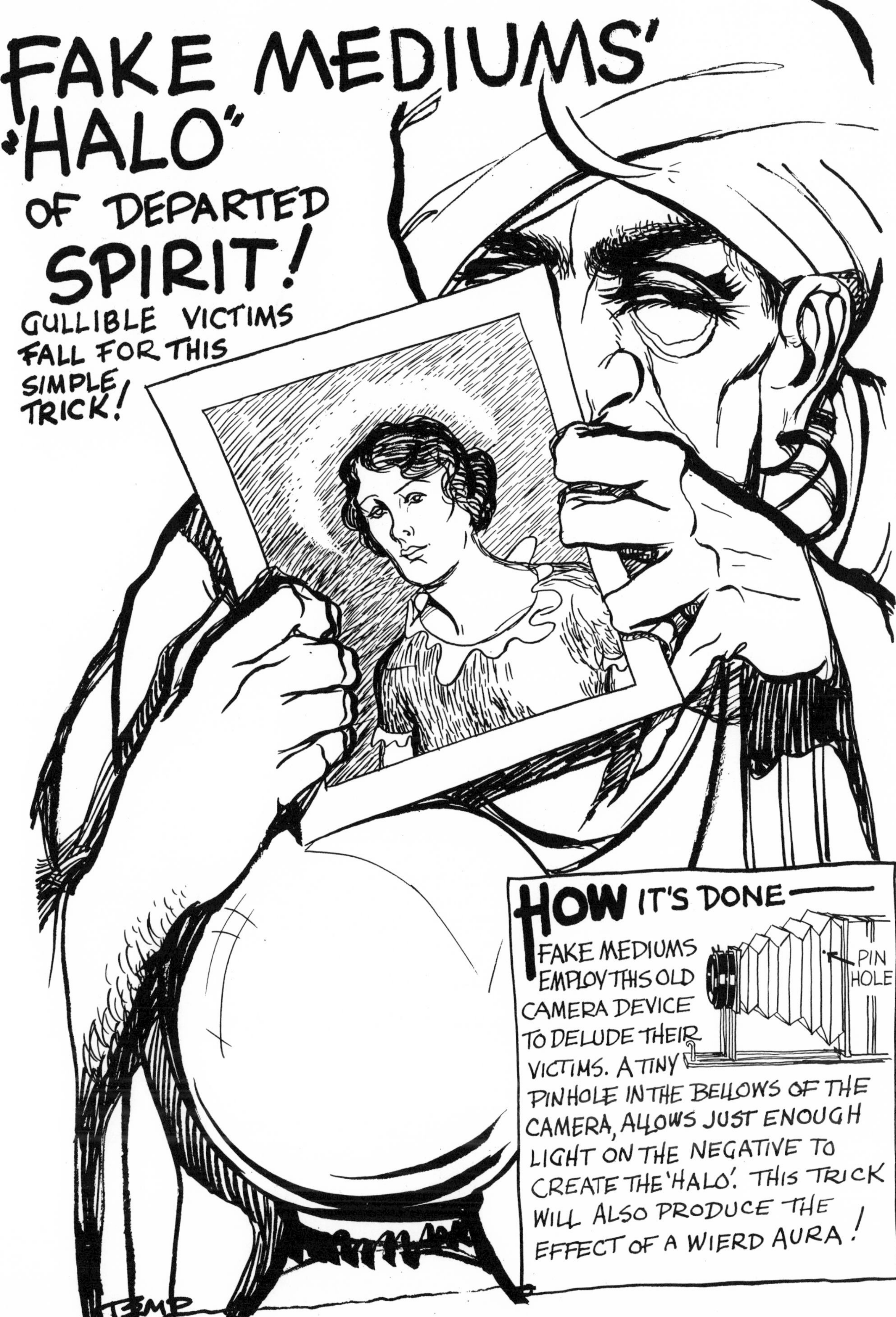
FAKE MEDIUMS'
"HALO"
OF DEPARTED
SPIRIT!
GULLIBLE VICTIMS
FALL FOR THIS
SIMPLE
TRICK!
HOW IT'S DONE—
FAKE MEDIUMS
EMPLOY THIS OLD
CAMERA DEVICE
TO DELUDE THEIR
VICTIMS. A TINY
PINHOLE IN THE BELLOWS OF THE
CAMERA, ALLOWS JUST ENOUGH
LIGHT ON THE NEGATIVE TO
CREATE THE 'HALO'. THIS TRICK
WILL ALSO PRODUCE THE
EFFECT OF A WIERD AURA!
PIN
HOLE
TEMP

THE FIRE WALKER!
JAPANESE PRIESTS MYSTERIOUSLY WALK BARE-FOOTED ACROSS BED OF FIRE!
HOW ITS DONE
THE SOLES OF THE FEET ARE COVERED WITH ALUM—AND PROPER TIMING IN THE WALK RENDERS THE WALKER IMMUNE TO THE FIRE!
'35

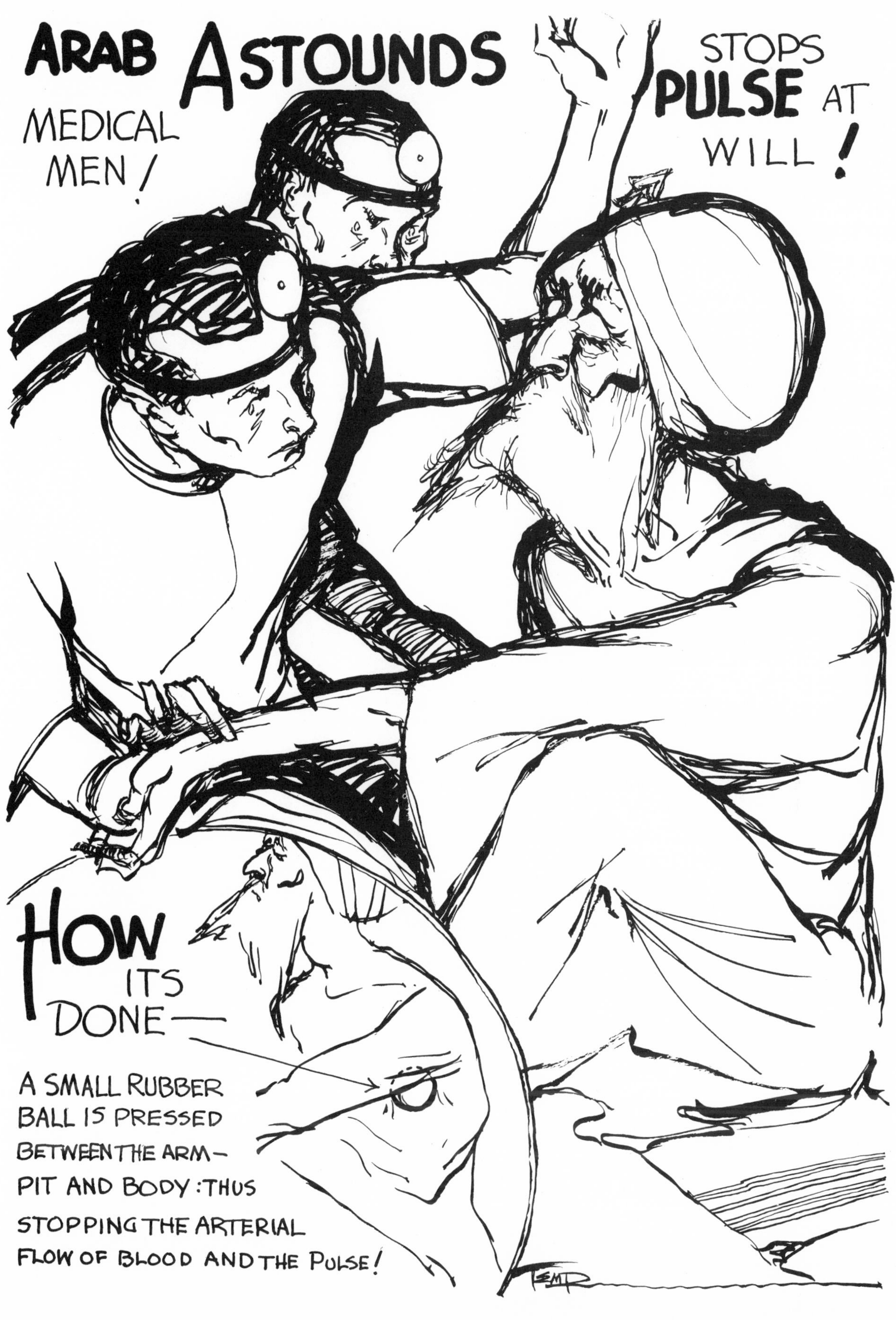
ARAB ASTOUNDS
MEDICAL MEN!
STOPS PULSE AT WILL!
HOW ITS DONE—
A SMALL RUBBER BALL IS PRESSED BETWEEN THE ARM-PIT AND BODY: THUS STOPPING THE ARTERIAL FLOW OF BLOOD AND THE PULSE!
TEMP

CONJURER RAISES FLOWERS—
BY COMMAND!
WATERS BARREN SOIL—AND FULL-GROWN PLANT MIRACULOUSLY APPEARS!
HOW IT'S DONE—
A HOLE IS FIRST DUG IN THE EARTH; FITTED INTO IT IS A CAN, LARGE ENOUGH TO HOLD THE PLANT, WHICH IS FIXED TO A CORK BASE, A BIT SMALLER THAN THE CAN. THE HOLE IS COVERED WITH TWIGS, BRANCHES, ETC. THE CORK, FLOATING ON THE WATER, THEN PUSHES THE PLANT UP—AND OUT!
TEMP

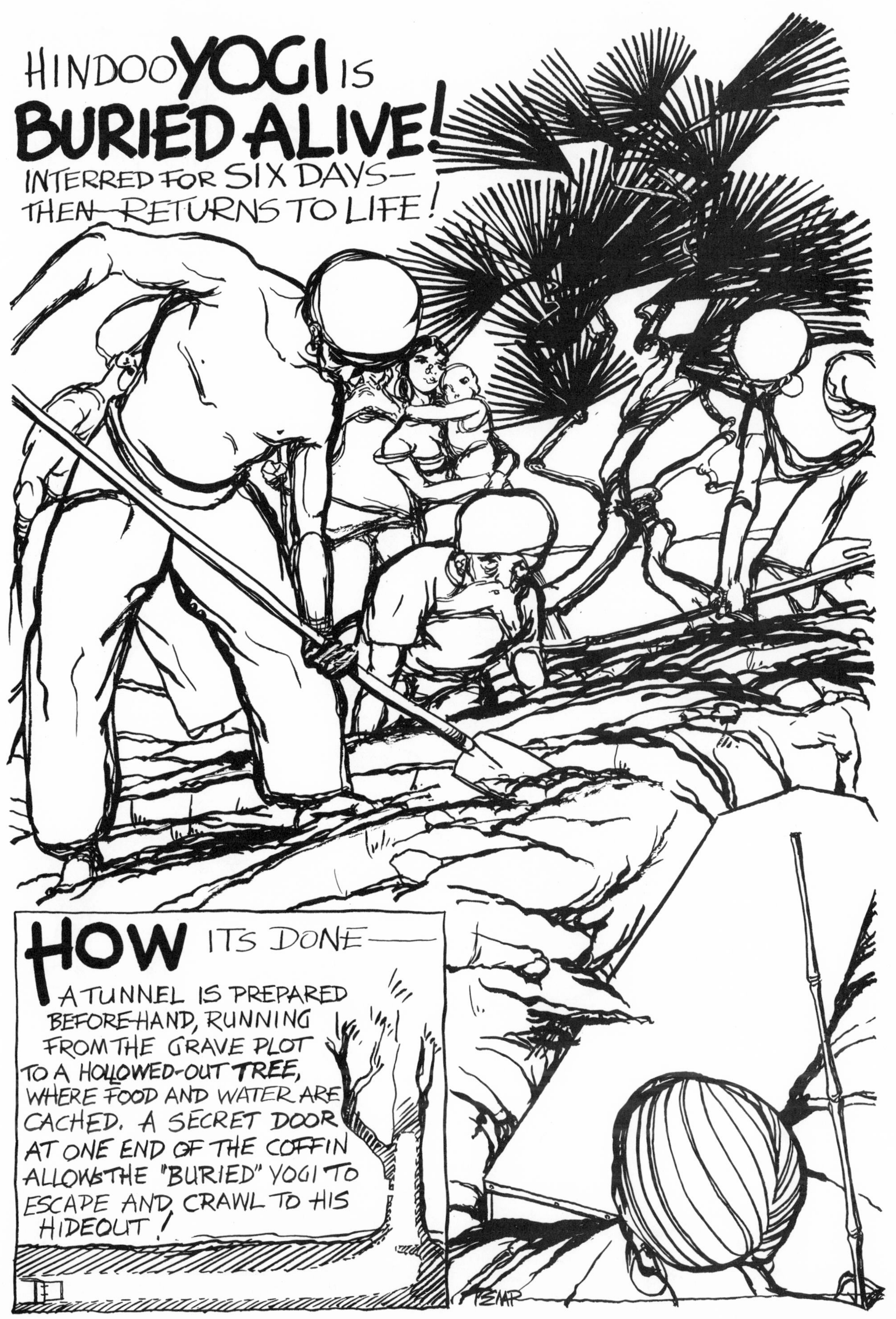
HINDOO YOGI IS BURIED ALIVE!
INTERRED FOR SIX DAYS—THEN RETURNS TO LIFE!
HOW ITS DONE—
A TUNNEL IS PREPARED BEFORE-HAND, RUNNING FROM THE GRAVE PLOT TO A HOLLOWED-OUT TREE, WHERE FOOD AND WATER ARE CACHED. A SECRET DOOR AT ONE END OF THE COFFIN ALLOWS THE "BURIED" YOGI TO ESCAPE AND CRAWL TO HIS HIDEOUT!

THE BOTTLE THAT TALKS!
SUSPENDED LEAD-WEIGHT INSIDE OF SEALED BOTTLE RAPS OUT "SPIRIT" ANSWERS TO QUESTIONS ASKED BY MEDIUM'S CLIENTS!
2 "PSYCHIC" RAPS MEAN 'NO'; 1 MEANS 'YES'—IN THE CODE OF THE "SPIRITS"
HOW ITS DONE—THE MEDIUM'S CONFEDERATE PRESSES ON A RUBBER BALL (A), HIDDEN UNDER THE CARPET. AIR PRESSURE, THRU THE CONNECTING TUBE TO RUBBER BALL (B) UNDER LEG OF TABLE, CAUSES FAINT MOVEMENT; WEIGHT SWINGS AND HITS BOTTLE!
B.
A.

MORE DARING THAN WILLIAM TELL! WITH AMAZING PRECISION, THE MODERN MAGICIAN SPLITS AN APPLE, RESTING ON A MAN'S NECK WITH ONE BLOW OF A SWORD!

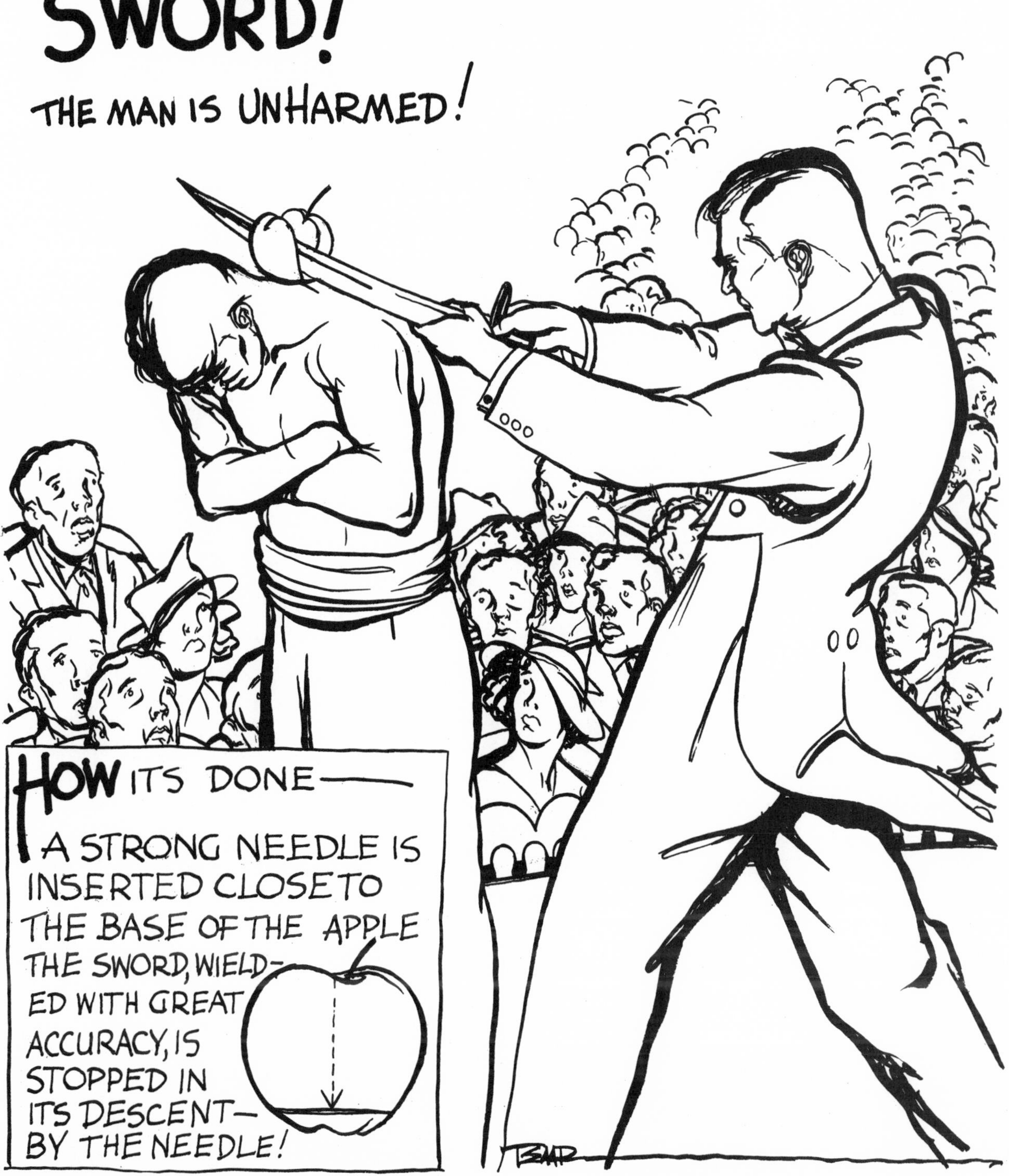

THE MAN IS UNHARMED!
HOW ITS DONE—
A STRONG NEEDLE IS INSERTED CLOSE TO THE BASE OF THE APPLE
THE SWORD, WIELDED WITH GREAT ACCURACY, IS STOPPED IN ITS DESCENT—BY THE NEEDLE!

WITCH-DOCTOR
MAKES WOODEN DUCK
SWIM BY COMMAND!
DUMBFOUNDS AFRICAN TRIBESMEN....
HOW ITS DONE
A TINY FISH IS TIED TO THE DUCK— WHICH RESTS ON THE TOP OF A TUB OF MUDDY WATER... WHEN THE HAND CASTS ITS SHADOW THE FISH, FRIGHTENED, DARTS TO AND FRO.
TEMP

MODERN MAGICIAN BALANCES A HALF-DOLLAR ON THE EDGE OF A SWORD!
ROLLS IT FORWARD AND BACK— IN UNBELIEVABLE FEAT OF BALANCE!
HOW IT'S DONE—
A DEVICE (A), MADE OF A THIN METAL DISK, THE SIZE OF A .50¢ PIECE IS SOLDERED TO A DISK THE SIZE OF A QUARTER, AND IS PALMED. THE HALF-DOLLAR (MARKED) IS FIXED TO THIS DEVICE BY A DAB OF BEESWAX MAKING WHEEL WITH A GROOVE, WHICH FITS OVER THE EDGE OF THE SWORD—BALANCING THE .50¢ PIECE-SO IT MAY ROLL FREELY!
(A.)
(B.)

THE STATUE SPEAKS!
WORSHIPERS TREMBLE AS EGYPTIAN GOD TALKS TO THEM!
HOW ITS DONE—
THE SUBTERRANEAN STREAM BENEATH THE GOD STATUE LEAVES LITTLE POOLS OF WATER IN THE NATURAL HOLLOWS AT THE BASE. AT NOON, THE INTENSELY HOT SUN OF EGYPT, SHINING THRU THE HOLE IN THE BACK, CAUSES THE WATER TO BOIL. THE SOUND IS AMPLIFIED BY THE INTERIOR GIVING OUT UNCANNY VOICELIKE SOUNDS!
TEMP

THE CIGARETTE THAT FLIES!
DUNNINGER MYSTIFIES THE (FORMER) PRINCE OF WALES – BY CAUSING A CIGARETTE TO FLY OUT OF HIS CASE!
HOW IT'S DONE—
ONE END OF A HAIR IS TIED TO THE VEST BUTTON. THE OTHER IS FIXED, BY A DAB OF BEESWAX, TO THE CIGARETTE. WHEN CAUGHT OVER THE FREE ARM, THE HAIR PULLS THE CIGARETTE OUT!
TEMP

NATIVE OF BRITISH WEST INDIES ASTOUNDS THE LATE KING GEORGE!
BLOWS A TRUMPET BY THE SIDE OF HIS NECK!
HOW ITS DONE
A SMALL RUBBER BALL IS ATTACHED TO A HORN (OLD AUTO TYPE), AND HELD IN PLACE BETWEEN THE ARM AND BODY—WHEN THE BALL IS SQUEEZED THE RESULTANT NOTE SOUNDS LIKE THE REAL THING!
TEMP

THE DAGGER TRICK!
HINDOO FAKIR PIERCES FACE THROUGH BOTH CHEEKS!
HOW ITS DONE
THE DAGGER IS IN 3 PIECES! THE SECTION IN THE MOUTH IS HELD AGAINST THE CHEEKS BY BRACES..... THE 2 OUTSIDE PIECES ARE CONNECTED & HELD IN PLACE BY A WIRE FITTED UNDER THE CHIN!
TEMP

IN TIBET
HE WALKS ON WATER!
HOW ITS DONE
THE MUDDY WATERS OF THE RIVER HIDE THIS INGENIOUS "WALK" OF TREE BARK TIED TOGETHER IN SECTIONS—THE TIBETAN MONKS BAFFLE THEIR FOLLOWERS WITH THIS ONE!
TEMP

CHINESE BUDDHIST RAISES WATER-SPOUT!
HOW ITS DONE
A TUBE, SUNK IN THE LAKE BED, IS RUN TO THE SMALL HOUSE ON SHORE;
A CONFEDERATE BLOWS AIR FROM A PUMP-THRU THE TUBE
THUS RAISING THE SPOUT!
TEMR